Magic Plants
Occult Botany

Magic Plants
Occult Botany

The secret constitution of plants, virtues of the medicinal herbs, hermetic medicine, philtres, ointments, magic drinks, tinctures, arcanes and spagyric elixirs.

Paul Sédir

OUROBOROS

Magic Plants Occult botany

© and translation 2020 by Daniel Bernardo

Translated from:
Les Plantes magiques. Botanique occulte...

ISBN: 978-1-989586-37-2

OUROBOROS

https://ouroboros.publiebook.com

Table of Contents

Part Two

PART THREE

APPENDIXES

To Papus

Allow me to dedicate this little essay to you, who first awakened my spirit to the facts of occultism.

In the twelve years since you first presented me with the spectacle of your work, many aspects of the science have passed before me, whose beauties and defects you have shown me. Today I am pleased to proclaim in public the great debt I have contracted with you. Heaven grant that, following your example, many workers may clear the ground where the Master of the Flock will gloriously pass.

Sédir
Epiphany, 1901

Preface to the first edition

The whole Universe is one great Magic, and the whole vegetable kingdom is animated by magical virtue; therefore, such a title as that of this little book would include, taken literally, the complete exposition of Botanology. Our ambition is not so high, and for good reason.

As in any study, there are two points of view in it: a lower, naturalistic and analytical one, and a higher, spiritualistic and synthetic one. Modern science deals with the former; we have chosen the latter because it is little known or largely forgotten today. Surely someone more authoritative will come along to present the third, the central one, the true point of view.

In short, in this essay there are less teachings than indications of study; the desire of those who read it will quickly and well complete all our imperfections.

PART ONE

The Vegetable Kingdom

In order to get the most accurate general idea possible of this kingdom, we must study it in itself, and then in its relations with the Universe and with Man. In this way, we will have the elements of a Botanogeny,[1] Physiology and Physiognomy (signatures) of plants.

Botanogeny deals with the cosmogonic principles whose interaction produces the kingdom in question.

Plant Physiology studies the living forces at work in plants.

Plant Physiognomy, the science of Signatures,[2] or the science of Correspondences, teaches us to recognise, from its external appearance, what is the quality of the forces acting in this or that plant.

---

1   Botanogeny deals with cosmogonic questions related to plants, while botany is the branch of biology that deals with the life of plants.

2   A natural external mark or symbolic appearance or characteristic of a plant, mineral or other object or substance indicating its special medicinal quality or its proper use.

§ I. – Botanogeny

As we have decided to bring to light, in this little book, only the traditional notions on the subject we are concerned with, we shall begin by presenting to the reader the most authentic teachings.

In the first place, one of the most ancient monuments we possess, the *Sepher* of Moses, will instruct us in the theories of the initiates of the red race and of the black race. Verse II of the first chapter of *Genesis* reads as follows:

> "Continuing with the declaration of His will, He/the Gods said: the Earth shall bring forth a herbaceous plant with an innate germ, a fruit-bearing substance, bringing forth its own fruit, according to its kind, and possessing in itself its own seed-power; and it was so."

This takes place on the third day according to the following correspondence:

Fire: 1st day: Creation of light.

Water and Air: 2nd day: Fermentation of the waters; their division.

Earth: 3rd day: Formation of the earth, its vegetation.

Fire: 4th day: Formation of the sun.

Water, Air: 5th day: Fermentation of water and air; birds and fish.

Earth: 6th day: Fermentation of the earth. – Animals and men.[3]

If we consider Genesis as a whole, the initiated rabbi will teach us that, from the cosmogonic point of view, the figure of Isaac represents the vegetable kingdom. His almost consummated sacrifice, his filiation, the names of his fathers and sons, and the acts of his symbolic life offer all the necessary proofs of this. In order not to weary our readers with too much arduous symbolism, we will not dwell on this study which any conscientious student can undertake.

---

3   According to A.F. Delaulnaye.

The Hermetic Theories

The Hermetic philosophers conceived, at the primordial origin of things, a *chaos* where the forms of the whole universe were prefigured, a cosmic matrix or matter, and, on the other hand, a generating *fire*, a source of all generation, whose reciprocal action constituted the monad, the stone of life, or *Mercury*, the medium and term of all forces.

This fire is hot, dry, masculine, pure; it is the Spirit of God borne upon the Waters, the Head of the Dragon, the *Sulphur*.

This chaos is a spermatic, feminine, hot, moist, impure water; the *Mercury* of the alchemists.

The action of these two principles in Heaven constitutes the good principle, the light, the heat, the generation of things.

The action of these two principles on Earth constitutes the evil principle, darkness, cold, putrefaction or death.

On Earth, pure fire becomes the great *limbus*, the *yliaster*, the *mysterium magnum* of Paracelsus, it is a vain and confused, damp earth, a moon, a mercurial water, the *Tohu v'bohou* of Moses. Finally, the pure and celestial water becomes a matrix, terrestrial, cold and dry, passive; the salt of the alchemists.

Thus, all things in Nature pass through three ages. Their beginning consists in the presence of their creative principles. This double contact produces light, then darkness, then confused and mixed matter; this is fermentation.

This fermentation leads to a general decomposition or putrefaction, after which the molecules of the working matter begin to coordinate according to their subtlety; this is sublimation, this is the life of the thing.

Finally, the time comes when this last work comes to an end; it is the third age; the separation is established between the subtle and the gross, the former goes to heaven, the latter to earth, the rest to the aerial regions. This is the end, death.

The passage of the four modes of the universal substance called the Elements; fire, earth and water are here easily recognisable, and we can coordinate all these notions by establishing a table of analogies which can be read by means of the Pythagorean triangle.[4] This procedure is found in India (Sankhya system) and in the Kabbalah (Tarot and Sephiroth).

Here are the principles at work in the three worlds, according to Hermetic terminology:

In the first world, the Spirit of God, the uncreated Fire fecundates the subtle and chaotic water which is the created light or soul of the bodies.

---

4   Cf. Papus, *Elementary Treatise on Occult Science.*

In the second world, this chaotic water, which is igneous and contains the sulphur of life, fertilises the medium water, that viscous, moist and unctuous vapour which is the spirit of bodies.

In the third world, this spirit which is elemental fire, fertilises the igneous ether which is still called thick water, slime, androgynous earth, the first solid and fecundated mixture.

Thus every earthly creature is formed by the action of three great series of forces: some from the empyrean heaven, some from the zodiacal heaven, and the last from the planet to which the creature belongs.

From the empyrean heaven come the *Anima Mundi*, the *Spiritus Mundi* and the *Materia Mundi*, viscous vapour, universal and uncreated seed.

From the zodiacal heaven come the sulphur of life, the intellectual mercury or ether of life and the salt of life or water of the beginning, created seed and second matter of bodies.

From the planet come elemental fire, elemental air, the vehicle of life, and elemental water, the receptacle of seeds and the innate seed of bodies.

Advent of the vegetable kingdom

The planet should be sufficiently evolved to produce water and an atmosphere, having crystallised its atoms to form a solid earth –as the account of Moses indicates–, to manifest on it the vegetable kingdom. Then a wave of new life descends, which is the vehicle of the first animation on the planet; it is therefore the symbol of beauty, and so the vegetable kingdom corresponds to Venus.[5] Therefore, it has the Spiral as its symbol, and that is why phyllotaxis can be used to measure the degree of vital force of each plant.

This plant life results from the reciprocal action of sunlight and the lust of the sulphur within; no plant can grow without the power of the sun which it attracts by its essential principle.

This is how the anonymous author of the *Light of Egypt* explains the evolution from mineral to plant:

Hydrogen and oxygen combined in water are polarised and form a substance which is the polar opposite of its primitive flammable state.

The heat of the sun decomposes again an infinitely small portion of the water; the atoms of this water molecule then adopt a differential motion which is that of the spiral. In this ascent, they attract the atoms of the carbonic acid and are attracted by them, hence a third movement occurs: a precipitous rotation. There, in new combinations, a germ of physical life is formed. Under the impulse

---

5   The greenness of the plants is the green sea from which Aphrodite emerged, fixed to the surface of the earth.

of a central fire atom, whose predominant forces are oxygen and carbon, this union produces another change of polarity whereby these atoms are again attracted to the earth. The water receives them and thus the first vegetative peat is formed. When these first vegetative forms die, these atoms resume their upward spiral walk, are attracted by the atoms of the air, and, by the same process of polarisation, succeed in forming successively more and more perfect lichens and plants.

> "The spiritual essence of the sun becomes, in the centre of the earth, by the attraction of each Mixture and by coagulation, a watery fire, and, wishing to return to its source, is retained, stimulating the matrices of various species. And as these matrices have a particular virtue in their species, one thing is determined in one, and in another a different thing, always engendering similar things… And if this spiritual essence is still more subtle, it passes to the surface of the earth, and makes the seeds grow according to their germ."[6]

The same theory is expounded in a more concise form in the Kabalistic treatise of the *Cinquante Portes de l'intelligence* (Fifty Gates of Intelligence). The enumeration of the Gates of the Decade of Mixtures is as follows:

1. Appearance of minerals through the disjunction of the earth.
2. Flowers and juices ordained for the generation of metals.
3. Seas, lakes and flowers, segregated between the alveoli.
4. Pasture and tree production.
5. Forces and seeds given to each of them, and so on.
6. Lastly, to conclude this brief presentation, let us state the theory of Jacob Boehme, whose identity with the two preceding ones will be easily discovered.

Created on the third day by the *Fiat* of *Mars*, which is bitterness, the source of motion, plants are born of the ray of fire in that bitterness. When God had separated the universal matrix and its igneous form, and wished to manifest Himself in this external and sensible world, the Fiat which came forth from the Father with His will, eternally proved the watery property of the sulphur of the prime matter; we know that Water, as an element, is an attractive matrix; therefore, we agree with the above theories.

Before the fall, the plants were united to the inner paradisiacal element; with the fall, sanctity fled from the root, which remained in the earthly elements; only the flowers represent, as we shall see later, paradise.

---

6   *Texte d'Alchymie*, Preface, p. 18. Paris, Laurent-d'Houry, 1695.

Static constitution of plants

Before we begin an outline of the physiology of plants, let us look for the principles at work in the vegetable kingdom in order to better understand how they function.

If we study plants from the point of view of their constitution, we will recognise five principles:

1. A matter, consisting of *vegetative Water*.
2. A Soul, made up of *sentient Air*.
3. A form of *concupiscent Fire*.
4. A womb, or *intellectual Earth*.
5. A universal and primitive essence, or *memory mixture*, formed by the four elements, determines the four phases of the movement: fermentation, putrefaction, formation and growth.

If we study it from the point of view of its generation, we find seven forces at work:

1. A matter, or patient, formed of light and darkness, chaotic and vegetative water; here are the *Derses* of Paracelsus, the hidden exhalation of the earth, by which the plant grows.
2. A form, active principle or fire.
3. A link between the two previous ones.
4. A movement, the result of the action of the agent on the patient. This movement, which is propagated by the four elements, determines the four phases we have enumerated above, on the memorable mixture. All this work, preparatory and hidden in a certain way, will produce visible results:
5. The soul of the plant, or bodily seed, the *clissus*[7] of Paracelsus, specific power and vital force.
6. The spirit or organised mixture, the *lephas*[8] of Paracelsus, or astral body of the plant.
7. The body of the plant.

To get a broader idea of these two classifications, analogies can be sought in the symbolism of Greek mythology, which is very expressive, offering ample material for meditation.

---

7 Paracelsus referred to the specific occult power contained in all things as *clissus*; the vital force which in vegetables ascends from the roots to the stem, leaves, flowers and seeds, causing the plant to produce a new organism.

8 *Lephas* is a hot vapour which, exhaling from the earth, is capable of making herbs and plants grow.

§ II. – Plant physiology

Anatomy

Nothing as simple as the structure of the plant. The anatomical parts are reduced to three, and it is these parts that will form, by individualising themselves, all the organs.

1. The general mass of the plant is formed by the *cellular tissue,* which may be regarded as the digestive organ of the plant (*root*: individualisation of the cellular tissues; intestine of the plant; seed [embryo]).

2. The spaces between the cells, usually hexagonal, form tubes that extend throughout the plant and carry the sap with which the plant is nourished. These tubes or intercellular ducts are to plants what blood vessels and veins are to animals (*stem*: individualisation of veins; plant blood system; capsule [female organ]).

3. In the cellular tissue of most plants, we observe other tubes formed by a spiral contour fibre that conducts air through the whole plant. These spiral tubes or vessels are to plants what the trachea is to animals. They are also called vegetable tracheae (*Leaves*: individual tracheae, the lungs of the plant).[9]

From this first sketch we will pass on to the functional relationship between these organs.

The embryological development of the plant includes the following phases:

1. Placement of the seed in a suitable matrix: moist soil.

2. The three parts of the germ begin to vegetate by feeding on the cotyledons.

3. The root begins to absorb nutrients from the soil. – The plant becomes individualised by its respiratory and digestive functions. It is born.

---

9   Oken, quoted by Dr. Encausse, *Anatomie philosophie*, Paris, p. 124.

This is, in essence, how Papus summarises plant physiology.[10]

1. *The Root*: sunk in the *Earth: stomach* of the plant; it will seek the nourishing *matter*;
2. *The Leaves*: rising in the free *Air* or dissolved in *Water: Lungs* of the plant. They seek the light and gases necessary for the renewal of the *force* that must drive the matter inside the tissues. This force is expressed through chlorophyll (green blood), mediating channels;
3. The *stem*: circulatory *apparatus*, whose vessels contain: 1° the *ascending sap* analogous to the chyle;[11] 2° the *air* absorbed by the lymphatic vessels specifically known as lactiferous]; 2° the *air* absorbed by the leaves; 3° the result of the action of the air on the nutritive sap, i.e. the *descending sap*.
4. *The flowers*: Surplus of strength; place of the reproductive apparatus.

We shall study these functions in a little more detail; on their knowledge depends, in fact, the whole art of hermetic pharmacopoeia, as we shall see in the second part of our study.

The seed is composed of:

1. The *germ* made up in turn of:
    a)   The raicile or radicle (future abdominal organs).
    b)   The shoot or germ (future respiratory organs).
    c)   The stalk (future circulatory organs, general centre of evolution). Analogous to the three sheaths of the human embryo.

2. The *cotyledons*: Materials destined to nourish the germ.

Each seed, which contains the potential tree, contains a *Mysterium Magnum*; consequently, in the development of the seed we find the inverted image of the creation of the world.

The tree begins to manifest itself as soon as the seed is placed in its natural womb, the earth.

However, the earth is only a passive matrix; therefore, it cannot develop the vital spark, nor ignite the *Being* of the seed so that the three principles of Salt, Sulphur and Mercury can manifest in it.

The light and heat of the Sun are necessary for this, for they move the cold subterranean fire. – Then the seed, involved in this development, undergoes its further evolution.

---

10 *Traité méthodologique de sciences occultes*, Ch. III, p. 267.

11 *Chyle* is a milky body fluid consisting of bile, pancreatic juice and emulsified lipids which is produced in the small intestine of humans and other vertebrates during the digestion of fatty foods, and is taken up by the lymphatic vessels specifically known as lactiferous.

In the second part, under *Agronomy – Cultivation of plants*, we will examine what happens when the matrix does not correspond to the seed entrusted to it.

Growth of the seed

Thus, we already see three *Beings*, three dynamisms in mutual reaction, each comprising its trinity of principles, *Salt, Sulphur* and *Mercury*: the *Being* of the earth, the *Being* of the seed and the *Being* of the sun. The first and the last *Beings* thus solicit, by a magnetic attraction, the development of the germ in two opposite directions; hence the root and the stem, which will play, as we know, in the life of the plant, similarly opposite roles.

The resulting harmony between these three *beings* depends on the good condition of the stem (smooth, green, or gnarled and black) and of the roots (multiple and fat or dry and fine).

Growth of the root

It is known that, from the point of view of the three principles, life and (magnetic) sensibility reside in the *Mercury*. The subterranean *Mercury* in the minerals is almost always poisonous and loaded with impurities; it is literally in hell, i.e. it finds no other food or object in its activity than itself.

As soon as a solar vibration reaches the *Mercury*, it engulfs it in its body, the *Salt*; and in its mother, the *Sulphur*, both of which are intimately united to its essence.

Then the earth opens up; its atoms obtain a relative freedom; and the plastic body, the *Salt*, which was in a saturnine stupor, becomes susceptible to attraction and is indeed attracted, in its homogeneous elements, by the *mind* of the germ.

Growth of the stem

Normally, the lower part of the stem is white, the centre is brown and the upper part is green.

The white indicates the tendency to sudden expansion of the constrictive powers of the root; the brown indicates a saturnine expression, the result of the divine curse; the bark is that part of the plant which is in limbo.

For if the Great Mystery is represented in the trees, the vegetable kingdom was reached, like the whole of Creation, by the fall of Adam; but in the beauty of the flowers and the sweetness of the fruits, we see, even more than in the other creatures, the splendours of Paradise.

Finally, green is the sign of the mercurial life which winds in the *Jupiter* and *Venus* of the foliage.

The tree

It is certainly the most perfect type of all vegetable beings; in it we find the influences of the stars, of the elements, of the *Spiritus mundi* and of the *Mysterium Magnum*, which is in itself Fire and Light, Wrath and Love, as the Word of the Eternal Father pronounces.

Nodes production

The bush grows by the mutual emulation of two *Beings*, the outer sun and the inner sun for the realisation of its end, which is the production of fresh water that will provide the flower with the elements of its elegant form and its beautiful colours.

It is known that the seven forms of outer Nature act thus in the plant: *Jupiter, Venus* and the *Moon* cooperate quite naturally with the expansive action of their inner Sun; but *Mars* exaggerates this expansion, for it is none other than the fiery spirit of *Sulphur, Mercurial* life swirls before it, and *Saturn* freezes and embodies this fright, thus nodes are produced.[12]

Branch production

The branches are the result of the struggle of the natural forces in full movement when they want to maintain communication with the sun outside; they are like the gesticulations of the plant that feels oppressed, and wants to enjoy the freedom of its own will. Just as the vital force of man causes the inner poisons to come out in the form of boils, so the vital warmth of the tree causes it to sprout, especially when the call of the outer *Being* is most urgent, as in spring.

In other words, to complete the explanation, the dread of mercurial life, or the *Salt* enclosed by ♄, struggles desperately, heats up, becomes *Sulphur*; this sulphur gives a new impulse to its child, *Mercury*; it tends to radiate; and ♀ gives it the plastic substance of buds and branches.

The flower

The *Sun* gradually overcomes the excesses of *Mars*; the plant diminishes its bitterness; *Jupiter* and *Venus* exhaust their activity and merge in the matrix of the *Moon*; the two unite so that the inner *Sun*, the vital force of the plant, recovers

---

12 In botany, the nodes are the areas of the stem from which the leaves grow. At this point of insertion, a leaf or the stem of a new twig develops, which sometimes gives rise to a more consistent bulge, which makes it possible to observe the nodes even when the leaf or twig has not yet developed.

its principle, passes into the state of *Azufre* and reintegrates the regime of divine freedom.[13]

The plant paradise

The seven forms are inverted, inside and out, in this very regime, and then enter into a play of complete harmony. The image of eternity is formed in time; the *Azufre* of the plant returns to the latent state; the *Salt* is transmuted: the reign of the Son is inaugurated with a paradisiacal joy, which is exhaled with perfume: thus the bodies of the saints give off an exquisite fragrance; this is what Paracelsus calls the *Tincture*.

The Seed

But as Adam sinned, this paradise soon ceases and returns to the darkness of the seed, where the two suns come to hide.

The Fruit

The hidden spirit of the elements operates in fruitfulness.

The fruits have a good and a bad quality, which they take from Lucifer. Therefore, they are not entirely under the regime of the Wrath, since the unique Word, which is immortal and incorruptible everywhere, even in the subterranean putrefaction of the seed, reverts in them; it is the Word that sustains the earth, but the earth has not captured the Word.

We have keep to the triumph of the regime of Love in the plant, that is, in its flowering. When it manifests, the *Being* is transported into place and, as a result, agglomerates a great number of plastic elements, i.e., moons, which the heat of the outer *Sun* transforms into *Venus*; thus the pulp of the fruit develops around a centre which is the child of the inner *Sun*. The seven planets are in the fruit and determine its taste; waiting for *Saturn* to bring it back down to Earth from where it had risen.

Ripening

The qualifier given to *ripe* fruits to designate their point of perfection, the period when their juice becomes sweet, is wrongly designated by this word which indicates, on the contrary, their state of agony. The English word *ripe*, the Ger-

---

13 Let us notice here two forms of inflorescence: the indeterminate, in which the growth starts from the centre, like the lily and the rose, symbolising spiritual development; and the determinate, in which the growth is from the circumference, symbolising material development.

man *reif*, the Arabic *ryp*,[14] the latter word being the metastasis of *pure*, are much more expressive.[15]

Maturation is the result of a kind of vertigo which the *Sun*, or the *mind*, makes the paternal principle of the *Sulphur* feel, and which precipitates it from eternal life into temporal life. From this we shall, in a moment, draw indications as to the meaning of the flavours of fruits.

Summary

We have made this quick sketch intentionally using all nomenclatures. We will repeat it in a few lines, using the following Buddhist or Ionian naturalistic theory .

We can consider the created world as the result of the interactions of three forces: expansion, light, or sweetness (Moses' Abel), contraction, darkness, or hardness (Cain), and rotation, anguish, or bitterness (Seth). We shall find these forces in the vegetable kingdom.

Let's assume the germ is placed in the earth. Sweetness flees from darkness and anguish, which pursue it; hence the growth of the plant.

In the heat of the sun, the struggle of the three forces becomes more ardent; contraction and rotation are exalted, they overwhelm expansion, hence the bark, the nodes.

But expansion, from the slightest respite left to it by its adversaries, spreads out on all sides and branches out, it is inscribed in the colour green and surrenders itself to the invigorating forces of the sun which bring it, in the flowers, to its perfection.

Contraction makes the various organs into a homogeneous whole, and distress divides them into parts, which cooperate with each other, because, coming from below, they must obey the solar force coming from above; thus the fruit is formed, which develops until the expansive energy is spent; at that moment it is ready to fall and give place to a new vital circulation.

The *od* of the plant

Since Reichenbach's discovery,[16] everything in Nature is known to emit a kind of exhalation invisible under ordinary conditions, but visible to the senses. This radiation varies in colour, intensity and quality.

---

14 Note that this word means something healthy, and also a *fetid purulent matter*, from *manure*.

15 Sédir compares here the French word *mûrs* (ripe, mature, ready) with their equivalents in other languages.

16 The Odic Force or od force, is the name given to a hypothetical vital force or energy put forward by the German Karl von Reichenbach in the middle of the 19th century. The term

The upper part of plants is always positive, and the lower part all the time negative, disregarding which fragment of the plant is presented to the sensitive.

Fruits are positive and tubers are negative.

In a fruit the flower side is positive, and the stalk side negative.

These observations are now used by the successors of Count Mattei, in the practice of electro-homeopathy; but personally I do not believe that this polarity is profound.

The soul of the plant

We take from a very well written book, by M.E. Boscowitz, the testimonies of scientists who attribute to the plant a life and a sensibility similar to that of a person. – Not to mention Brahmanic, Buddhist, Taoist, Egyptian, Platonic and Pythagorean doctrines, all of which are more or less impregnated with the spirit of initiation, we must remember that philosophers such as Democritus, Anaxagoras and Empedocles have defended this thesis. In more modern times, Percival states that root movements are voluntary; Vrolik, Hedwig, Bonnet, Ludwig, and F. Ed. Smith assert that the plant can experience sensations, that it can know happiness; Erasmus, and Darwin in his *Botanical Garden*, says that it is animated; the works of Von Martius[17] prove the same; Theodore Fechner finally wrote a book entitled: *Nanna oder uber das Seelenleben der Pflanzen*.

The analogy between plants and beings with personality is the following:

Breathing takes place through Malpighi's tracheae, which is a spiral ribbon of cells, which coils up in a spiral and has the ability to contract and expand.

Air is indispensable to its life (experiences of Calandrini, Duhamel, Papin); and it exerts on the sap an action similar to that which it has on the blood (Bertholon).

The underside of the leaves is perforated with stomata, organs of respiration (Exp. d'Ingenhous, de Hales, Théodore de Saussure, de MM. Mohl and Garreau).

Leaves retain oxygen from the air and exhale carbonic acid (Garreau, Hugo Von Mohl, Sachs).

They feed on carbon, which they extract from carbonic acid, so they exhale a large amount of oxygen during the day.

Their roots serve as stomachs, as do their leaves; the sap is similar to chyle.

Plant nutrition is such an active function that Bradley calculated that an oak tree absorbs 280,000 kilograms of food in a hundred years.

---

is derived from Odin, a Norse mythological god.

17 See *Reise in Brasilien; Pflanzen und Thiere des tropischen America; Die Unsterblichkeit des Pflanzen*.

Almost all plant excretions are life-giving substances for humans, just as animal excretions are life-giving substances for plants.

If the circulation of sap is not yet a proven fact, it is at least known that plants transpire a lot.

How can we explain the movement of plants in search of light, sun and food, i.e. a favourable environment?

How can we explain their power of love, the heat, the electricity they give off when they fertilise?

Finally, where do the marvellous properties of the resurrection flower and the Rose of Jericho come from?[18]

The Initiate is aware of all these phenomena and admires once again the ingenious wisdom of his predecessors, as well as the penetrating intuition of the peoples who gave to each tree its Hamadryad,[19] to each flower its fairy, to each herb its genie. Do not the scientific observations just summarised show with truthfulness the obscure movements of the souls of the elementals that strive for consciousness?

Plants and animals

The ingenious Bonnet, of Geneva, devotes the whole tenth part of one of his books[20] to the parallelism of plants and animals; and he expresses the result of his numerous comparisons as follows:

> "Nature descends by degrees from man to the polyp, from the polyp to the sensitive, from the sensitive to the truffle. The higher species always have, by their character, something of the lower species; and the latter of the still lower species… The *organised* matter has received an almost infinite number of diverse modifications, and they are all shaded like the colours of the prism. We make dots on the image, and draw lines on it; we call this making genus and classes. We see only the dominant tints, and the delicate shades escape us.

> "So plants and animals are only modifications of organised matter. They all partake of a common essence, and the distinguishing attribute is unknown to us."[21]

Plants vegetate, feed, grow, and multiply; but the seeds of plants are much more numerous than the fertilised eggs or ova in animals, except in the lower species.

---

18 The Rose of Jericho is one of the plants included in the *Little Dictionary of Botany* included in this book.

19 *Hamadryads* are forest Nymphs, who are born and die with the trees.

20 *Contemplation de la nature*, vol. II.

21 *Ob. cit.* in volume II, chap. xxxiv. p. 84.

Similarly, an individual produces many more shoots in the first kingdom than foetuses in the second.

Food is absorbed through porous surfaces in some species and through a single mouth in others; feeding through the outer roots is incessant; in developed animals, it is done at intervals and through the inner roots (water vessels).

Most plants are hermaphrodites.

Plants are immobile, except for the movement of leaves and some flowers towards the sun; animals are mobile.

General conclusion

The result of this rapid study shows us that the general movement of terrestrial life in these three lower kingdoms appears as the gigantic effort of an organised Power (physical Nature) towards free will, passing from the immobility characteristic of the mineral kingdom to individualisation (plants), and then to spontaneous movement (animals).

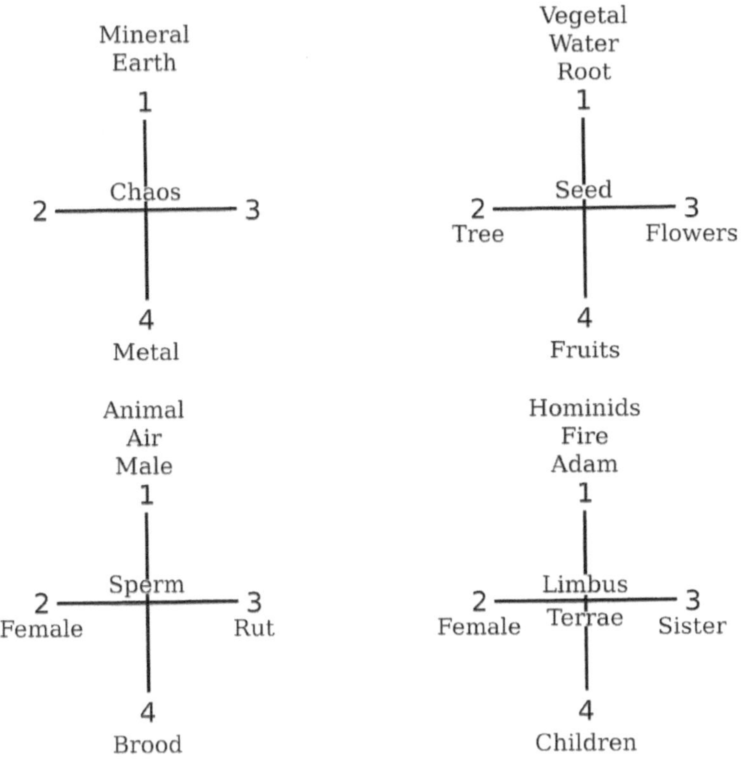

This is strikingly expressed in the four diagrams shown in the previous page, completed by Madathanus, which allow us to consider each kingdom as a medium whose atoms are in a particular phase of motion at rest, then in a state of equilibrium, then in a state of whirlwind, then in resolution.

The fifth, sixth and seventh states represent the realms (spiritual for us) higher than the present evolution of the human race.

§ III. – THE SIGNATURES

(Vegetal Physiognomy)

Each plant is an earth star. Its celestial properties are inscribed in the colours of the petals, and its terrestrial properties in the shape of the leaves; all Magic is contained in them, for the plants represent all astral powers.

There are three different keys to recognise the inner virtues of a plant from its outer properties: the binary key, the quaternary, elemental or zodiacal key, and the septenary or planetary key.

Binary key

Here, according to Saint-Martin, is the theory with two examples of practical application.

"There is in every thing, whether material or immaterial, an impulsive force, which is the principle from which that thing receives its existence…

"But this universal impulsive force which we observe in nature would not be produced if a compressive, opposing like force were not pressing upon it, so as to increase its intensity; it is this force which, by stimulating it, causes, at the same time, the development and appearance of all the properties and all the forms generated by the impetus of the impulsive force.

"Vegetation, mainly, offers us these two laws clearly, in all its different activities. In the kernel of a fruit, resistance prevails over force, and so it remains inactive; when it has been planted, and vegetation is established, that only happens because force combats resistance and is balanced by it. When the fruit appears, it is the force that has prevailed over the resistance and has succeeded in overcoming all obstacles, though this fruit is nevertheless offered to us only as the union of force and resistance, in its composition and its substantialised properties, and its envelope which contains, gathers, preserves and corroborates them, according to this universal law of things.

"From this picture we can see what wounds have been inflicted on primitive and eternal nature, which we have recognised as the prerogative of man.[22]

"The object of vegetation –explains this adept in the continuation of the same work–, is to transmit to us the rays of beauty, colour and perfection which have their source in the higher region, and which only tend to penetrate our lower region.

"Every grain of seed is a little chaos.

"Everything in nature is composed of a divisible action, force, and of a divisible action, resistance.

"When the latter is deprived of the former, it produces water; when not, it produces fire.

"Just as the union of fire and water is manifested in the green colour of the leaves, so putrefaction is located in the roots, and sublimation in the bright colours of flowers and fruits.

"The seeds, being the prison of the higher powers, take up in an analogous way the story of the fall and the myth of Saturn devouring his children.

"Thus generation is a struggle whose phases are expressed by the signature, and there is no being that does not tell, by its external form, the story of its own birth…

"…In the oak, the bitter and austere kernel, enclosed in its acorn, indicates that this tree has undergone a violent effort of resistance, an effort which tended nothing less than to destroy it…

"If with this same gaze we consider the leaf of the vine, the seed of the grape and the properties of the wine, we shall soon recognise that in the seed, the water has been extremely concentrated by the resistance, so that it develops so abundantly in the branches of the vine;

"That in this expansion of water, the vine-leaf indicates, by its form, that it is so abundant only because it has been separated from its fire, and that its factors have been binary as in an infinity of other plants;

"That, consequently, the fire has been so extremely separated from the water, as is known in the branch of the vine, where the leaves and the peduncle of the raceme alternate together, but always on the opposite side;

"That, according to its law, this fire always rises higher than the water, which is made known to the peduncle of the raceme, which always rises above its corresponding leaf;

"That also this fire is very close to the primitive life, which is as one with it, whereby the grape acquires such a regular spherical form, as if it had pumped through its stamens and pistil the full circle of astral virtualities,

---

22 Saint-Martin, *L'esprit des choses*, vol. I, p. 140.

the number of which covers the whole circumference and establishes the balance between endurance and strength;

"That, for this reason, it is so wholesome and salutary when taken in measure and moderation;

"But that, in view of the divided or binary source from which it is derived, it must cause the greatest havoc when taken in excess;

"That, moreover, these excesses are of a remarkable kind: 1st because they lead to strife, to absence of reason, to quarrels and murders; 2nd because they lead to lust, which is written in so many ways in the form of the seed; 3rd because drunkenness, by exciting lust, is nevertheless far from being fatal to the Generation."[23]

Elementary classification

We know that each of the four elements with the quintessence corresponds to each of our five senses; that is to say, each of these five forms of movement reveals to us the qualities of objects by a vibration of one of our sensory nerve centres.

Earth corresponds to the olfactory sense (smell).

Water corresponds to taste (flavour).

Fire corresponds to sight (form).

Air corresponds to touch (volume).

Quintessence corresponds to hearing (spirit).

Hence the following table.

Table Nº 1					
Plants	Flower smell	Fruit taste	General form	Colour	Volume
of Earth	Intense	Sweet	Compact	Yellow	Small
of Water	Null	Acid	Creeping	Greenish	Small stalk Bit leaves and fruits
of Fire	Strong	Hot	Twisted	Red	Medium Expansive
of Air	Bad	Astringent	Slender	Bluish	Very high

---

23 *L'esprit de choses*, vol. I, pp. 156 and 199.

This includes only the simple types, which are purely theoretical; in reality, these four elements must be combined together and we obtain the table N° 2 of the zodiac signs, which can indicate the general character of a plant.

If, now, we want to know *a priori* the qualities of a plant signed, for example, by Aries, by referring to this last table, we see that Aries is a fire (vertical col.) of earth (horizontal col.). The qualities of this plant will therefore be, according to the first chart, a pungent and intense smell, a pungent taste with nothing unpleasant; the flowers will be orange–red; and the plant will be small, though robust.

Table N° 2 – Zodiacal signatures				
	Fire	**Earth**	**Air**	**Water**
Water	Fire	2 Taurus	3 Gemini	4 Cancer
Earth	1 Aries	Earth	7 Libra	8 Scorpio
Air	5 Leo	6 Virgo	Air	12 Pisces
Water	9 Sagittarius	10 Capricorn	11 Aquarius	Water

We believe that this example will be sufficient for the understanding of this method; here are the signatures of each of the zodiacal signs, compiled according to a large number of authors, so that we can perfect them in practice.

The plants signed by *Aries* will be hot and dry; the Fire element will dominate them; finally, their conformation will offer more or less distant resemblances to the head and its subdivisions: eyes, nose, tongue, teeth, beard; they have yellow flowers, pungent taste, thin stem and leaves, diphyllous or bipetalous. *Perfume*: myrrh.

Plants signed by *Taurus* are cold and dry; the Earth element dominates; their taste is therefore sour, with a sweet smell, they are tall, give off aromatic fragrances, freeze easily, bear many fruits. There are some which are shaped like a throat; androgynous flowering plants. *Perfume*: balsamite (*Tanacetum balsamite*).

Gemini plants are warm and moderately humid, their element is Air; they are herbs with white or pale flowers, very green, mild flavoured, often milky; they have a certain conformity of figure with the shoulders, arms, hands, udders; they are often hetaphilous. *Perfume*: mastic (*Pistacia lentiscus*).

Plants signed by *Cancer* are cold and wet; water dominates: they are insipid, marshy, with white or ashy flowers; they often grow at the water's edge; their leaves take the shape of lungs, liver or spleen; they are spotted, swollen, with five petals. *Perfume*: camphor.

Plants signed by *Leo* are warm and dry, dominated by the Fire element; they have red flowers, or a sharp or bitter taste, or very fast burning; their fruit has the shape of a stomach or heart; cruciferous. *Perfume*: incense.

Plants signed by *Virgo* are cold, dry and contain a lot of earth. They are creeping plants, with hard, brittle tissues, whose leaves and roots resemble the abdomen or intestines. In the vast majority of cases, their flowers have five petals. *Perfume*: white sandalwood.

Plants signed by *Libra* are warm, moist and airy; their flowers are tawny, their stems tall, soft and flexible; their fruits or leaves resemble the shape of the kidneys, the navel, the bladder, their taste is sweet; they grow preferably on stony ground. *Perfume*: galbanum.

Plants signed by *Scorpio* are warm and moist. They can be tasteless, watery, viscous, milky or fetid, and have the shape of a man's sexual organs. *Perfume*: red coral.

Plants signed by *Sagittarius* are hot and dry; dominated by the fire element; they are bitter, and take the forms of the anal region. *Perfume*: aloe.

Plants signed by *Capricorn* are cold and dry; they are dominated by the earth element; their flowers are greenish, their juice coagulates and is toxic. *Perfume*: tuberose.

Plants signed by *Aquarius* are moderately warm and humid; they are also aerial and very often aromatic: they take the form of legs. *Perfume*: euphorbium.

Plants signed by *Pisces* are cold and damp; water seems to dominate them; their taste is insipid, their shape is that of fingers; they grow in cool, dark places, at the water's edge. *Perfume*: thyme.

Septenary or planetary classification

Here are, in a nutshell, the basis of the classification:

Saturn: astringent, concentrator.

Jupiter: radiant, majestic.

Mars: choleric, thorny.

Sun: beauty and nobility, harmony.

Venus: sweet.

Mercury: indeterminate.

Moon: strange.

By developing these characters, we have:

Table № 3				
	General form	**Flowers**	**Perfume**	**Fruits**
Saturn	Big and sad	Black, grey	Stinky	Pungent, poisonous
Jupiter	Large, leafy	Blue or white, joyful	Odorless	Sweet, acid
Mars	Small, thorny	Red, small	Pungent and unpleasant	Warm, hot, peppery, poisonous
Sun	Medium	Yellow	Aromatic	Acids, good
Venus	Small, flowery	Roses, beautiful, large	Delightful, heavy	No fruits or sweet
Mercury	Medium, convoluted	Small, variegated	Piercing or bad	Mixed flavour
Moon	Strange	White	Odorless or bland	Insipid, disgusting

The taste is given by the *salt* of the earth where the plant grows; it indicates the ideal of the plant and the path to follow to extract the balsam.

The leaves and stem indicate the dominant planet.

In a plant:

The root is from Saturn;

The seed and bark of Mercury;

The strong wood, from Mars;

The leaves, of the Moon;

The flowers, of Venus;

The fruit, of Jupiter.

Planetary Signatures

Plants signed by *Saturn* are heavy, glutinous, astringent, bitter, pungent or acetic; roots, plants which produce fruit without flowers, which produce without seeds, which are rough, with black berries; which have a pungent smell, a frightful shape, a sinister shade, which are resinous, narcotic, dedicated to the funerary, and which grow slowly.

Plants ruled by *Jupiter* have a sweet, mild, subtle, styptic and even sour taste; all plants that bear fruit, even without flowers; those that are very fruitful and rich in appearance.

Plants ruled by *Mars* are sour, bitter, pungent and hot; they are poisonous when heated; they are prickly, stinging to the touch or irritating to the eyes.

The *solar* plants are aromatic, pungent in taste; they ward off lightning and are counter-poisons; there are also some that remain evergreen; they are good for divination and against evil spirits; they turn towards the sun or bear its figure in their leaves, flowers or fruits.

Plants ruled by *Venus* have a sweet, pleasant and mild taste; they produce flowers without bearing fruit; they have many seeds and are aphrodisiacs; their smell is almost always sweet.

Plants corresponding to *Mercury* have a mixed taste; they produce flowers and leaves without fruit; the leaves are small and the colours are varied.

Plants ruled by the *Moon* are tasteless, they live by or in water; they are cold, milky, narcotic, anti-aphrodisiac, their leaves are usually large.

Friends and enemies of plants according to their sign.

Friendly signs:
Taurus: Cancer and Sagittarius.
Gemini: Libra and Aquarius.
Cancer and Libra.
Virgo: Taurus.
Scorpio: Cancer.

Enemy signs:
Taurus: Libra, Scorpio.
Gemini: Capricorn.
Cancer: Sagittarius.
Virgo: Aries and Leo.

Enemy planets:
Saturn, Mars, Sun.

Friendly planets:
Venus with all, especially Mars.
Mercury with all, especially Jupiter.

Combinations of influences

Here are some examples, to help the student, of the results of the combined influences of various planets:

Saturn dominant, for example, gives a black or dirty grey plant, with a hard, rough stem, sour or salty taste; large and slender, with dark flowers; it almost always calls to *Mars*, and then the plant becomes uneven, gnarled, branched, wild and tormented looking.

Saturn and *Venus* give a great tree, strong because the sweetness of Venus gives the matter to develop the sulphur of Saturn.

If *Jupiter* is near *Venus*, the plant is full of strength and virtue.

If *Mercury* influences a plant between *Venus* and *Jupiter*, it is even more perfect; it is a beautiful, medium-bodied plant, with white or blue flowers.

If the *Sun* is close to the above, the flower turns yellow.

If *Mars* is not contrary, the plant is able to resist all bad influences, and gives excellent remedies. But such a combination is very rare, because it is close to Paradise.

If *Mars* and *Saturn* are contradictory, together with *Mercury*, *Venus* and *Jupiter*, it is a poisonous tree, with reddish flowers and a white tinge (because of Venus), rough to the touch and with a terrible taste.

If, although *Mars* and *Saturn* contradict each other, *Jupiter* and *Venus* are powerful, and *Mercury* is very weak, the plant is warm and healing; the stem is thin, a little rough and thorny; the flowers are whitish.

If *Venus* is close to *Saturn*, if the *Moon* does not oppose *Mars* and *Jupiter*, free, it gives a pretty, tender, delicate plant, with white flowers, harmless but not very useful.

PART TWO

Man and Plants

he vegetable kingdom, subject to *Venus*, has only one function in relation to man: to nourish him.

The plant can nourish man, i.e. it can repair organic losses:

1. In his physical body, i.e. by nourishing it.

2. In his electromagnetic body, i.e. by curing his illnesses.

3. In its astral body: sleepwalking, ecstasy, magic ceremonies, divination.

Man, in turn, can do three things for the plant:

1. Cultivate it (magical agriculture).

2. Redeem it (magical growth).

3. Resurrect it (palingenesis).

We shall study each of these six articles separately.

§ I. – Nutrition

I do not want to repeat here a plea for vegetarianism; more knowledgeable scholars than myself have authoritatively pointed out its advantages. Let me point out a few rules for novice vegetarians.

1. Pass slowly from creophagy[1] to vegetarianism, and change fermented drinks, for milk or water, only when the change of diet to solid food is accomplished; this change should be aided by an increased consumption of fleshy or watery fruits.
2. Carry out this dietary change in the countryside.
3. Practise vegetarianism in the cities, and especially in big cities like Paris, only if you does not eat in restaurants, and if you don't have general debility.
4. Don't worry about eating a greater quantity of plant foods than the animal foods one used to eat.
5. Keep fish for a long time in your meals; eggs, milk and butter should never be excluded, except in exceptional cases of asceticism.
6. Lastly, learn at the same time to govern little by little your physical organism and to become master, using your own free will, of the small functional irregularities which may arise.

How to take meals

In general, the more energy we expend to perform an act, the more profitable that act will be for us. – Thus, taking things to the extreme, we should grow our food plants ourselves, harvest them and prepare them ourselves, in utensils that serve only these purposes. For the naturalistic and pantheistic initiations, which develop the student from the bottom upwards, or from the outside in, begin by purifying and perfecting the astral body and finally the intelligence.

---

1   Carnivorous nutrition.

Thus it is that Hindu Brahmins and ascetics are instructed to prepare their food themselves, and never let others touch the copper utensils except their wives.

From this also come prescriptions concerning the position of the body during eating; there are relations between the electromagnetic currents of a planet and those of the individuals living on its surface; it would be too long to expound this theory here; let us confine ourselves to saying that it is best for our countries to eat facing North.

Another prescription is that of ablutions; Hindu priests wash their hands, feet, mouth, nose, eyes and ears, repeating a sacred invocation. In our country, this corresponds to the *Blessing of the table* which, when pronounced magically, i.e. from the depths of the heart, has a real invigorating value.

Finally, a last prescription is that of silence; it is observed among religious throughout the world; its purpose is, by concentrating the attention on the act of eating, to reduce, in sensible proportions, the quantity of matter necessary for reparation; digestion thus requires less activity of the solar plexus, hence the economy of nervous force which the exercises of contemplation fruitfully employ. – But for those who live in and with the world, in the heavy atmosphere of the great cities, joy is the best digestive, and is worth more than all the spirits of the world, to stimulate the sluggishness of the stomach.

§ II. – Therapeutics

The curative virtues of the vegetable kingdom have always been the most famous; and that was always the most common idea among men; the Greek name of the god of medicine himself, *Esculapius*, means: the forest, hope of salvation, or according to Porphyry, the solar faculty of regenerating bodies, or that which repairs the solutions of continuity in the tissues.

Plants can be used in medicine in their three states: living, dead or resurrected.

The living plant serves as a modifier of the environment, but especially when it is aromatic. Its scent then invigorates all the respiratory mucous membranes, acting as an anti-inflammatory. Thus, it will do tuberculosis sufferers good to breathe in the scent of pine, lavender, rosemary, basil, mint, etc.

This is the exoteric use of living plants; their esoteric use is indicated by Paracelsus under the name of *transplantation of diseases*.

Transplantation of diseases

Diseases can be transplanted from the sufferer to any other living being.

This practice, although recommended by the moral authority of the great masters of occultism, is pernicious to the spiritual plane of both man and plant.

For ulcers and wounds, persicaria (*Persicaria maculosa*), comfrey (*Symphytum officinale*), *Botanus europeus*, etc., are used.

For toothache, rub the gums until they bleed with ragwort root (*Senecio vulgaris*).

For uterine menorrhoea, take mumia[2] with persicaria seeds (*Persicaria maculosa*).

For *menorrhœa difficili*, pennyroyal (*Mentha pulegium*).

For pulmonary consumption, oak or cherry.

---

2   In alchemy, *mumia* refers to an amalgam of lead and mercury. Here the name is applied to spirits supposedly present in corpses, to which virtues were attributed for the cure of various diseases.

Nowadays, medicinal substances have been experimented with the action at a distance on hypnotic subjects: see in this respect the work of Dr. Bourru, Burot, Luys, Professor Durville and the magnetisers of the first half of the 19th century.

I give here only isolated examples, the student can multiply them at will according to the laws of signatures.

The collected plants can be used exoterically:

- In juice.
- In powder.
- In infusion.
- In decoction (boiled in water); more active than infusion.
- In magistral preparations.
- In tincture (in alcohol).
- As a quintessence.

Here are some practical indications on this external pharmacopoeia, taken from the books of some ancient doctors; you will find in these books manipulations of the modern pharmacopoeia that everyone can reproduce at home.

For a herbal medicine is always more active if it is prepared by a person who is strong and eager to heal. This is one of the secrets of the success of homeopathic pills and dilutions.

I knew an old St. George's district health officer who used to cure the most stubborn dyspepsia with breadcrumbs; only he spent two or three hours every day kneading them himself in his pharmaceutical laboratory.

Tinctures, decoctions, powders, etc.

Take, for example, hellebore, tar and hemlock.

"A popular error that has prevailed is that hellebore is intended only for insanity, although it also serves to cure and prevent many evils, and even to preserve and prolong life, if one considers carefully its efficacy and virtue, which serve to renew Nature, rectify the blood and purge the impurities whose excess, retardation and suppression cause much discomfort in our days. Antiquity has happily practised it, and in our days it has been too much forgotten, to the detriment of the public, for whose relief the hellebore should be restored to its former dignity.

"…As an alternative, it is convenient to take the black hellebore of Theophrastus (*Helleborus niger*), the most singular and safe among the species, according to the opinion of those who for many years have been engaged in medicine: in view of its milder and more favourable effects than many, such as the hellebore of Dioscorides, the white hellebore, eleborine or false hellebore, and others, notwithstanding the trials that have been made with them, or even with the white.

"…We can take the root of the black hellebore, cut it and stuff an apple with it, which will be aerated at night, in the morning we will cook the apple slowly, take out the root, pulverise it, obtaining half a shield[3] of weight, three hours before eating. This is to be repeated three or four times a year, mainly in autumn and spring.

"This is a clear precaution for the evacuation of the dirt from the body, from which the most annoying indispositions are born; we will increase the dose if we wish to do so.

"The leaves and root of hellebore may be boiled in rye bread for correction, in powder, the ingestion is thirty and forty grains,[4] and more for the stout, either in pill, or with wafers, baked apple, or other form, two hours before the broth.

"The whole plant may also be pulverized, the weight already mentioned, without any preparation, as was done in Rome.

"The root may be counted and cooked with the pulp, in the form of broth, consommé, jelly, or tincture, of which some time will be taken to have a gentle purge, though it is lawful to add some ingredient if desired, to improve its flavour.

"Some, to better obtain the end of renewal and drainage of the blood, will gradually, and imperceptibly, accustom themselves to the use of black hellebore leaves gathered in a good season, dried in the shade with an equal portion of sugar; it is a means of attaining a great age free from various diseases, both internal and external to the last breath of life.

"The starting point is from 10 to 15, a maximum of 20 grains; so that from gradually it comes to 30 grains daily, for some time, finally reaching one drachm.[5] But it should only be taken in that form from six days to six, so that hellebore becomes ordinary and familiar, thus losing its purgative force it is only renewing and rectifying.

"It is reduced to balsam by the industry of the artisan; the dose of this balsamic virtue is ten grains.

"A very excellent quintessence is thus obtained, which surpasses all previous preparations of hellebore in artifice and renovating goodness, the ingestion of which is from five to six drops with some suitable liquor, such as lemon balm water, agar or pulp quintessence.

---

3   A coin, the old French crown, or ecu, having on one side the figure of a shield.

4   Pharmacy term. A name sometimes given to preparations differing from pills only by their globular form. Its weight was 0.0532 grams.

5   5.1 grams.

"From the whole plant, well washed and watered with sour wine, a syrup is made to purge the black and earthly humour, or to put it well, to separate the pure from the impure, and the noxious, and to uproot the evils proceeding thence and from its continuance, this syrup operates more surely and benignly than other purgatives; I prefer this syrup to the extract; though the two, both syrup and extract, have no other effect than to purge from beneath, they are not strong enough to rectify the blood and keep the health in a firm and steady state.

"I ascribe to the prolonged use of this plant, chiefly in its root, a wonderful action in loosening and untying the cords of capital diseases, in addition to and over and above the distinguished faculty of renewing the body, rectifying the blood, or purging decay, which often causes health to decay or perish, so that it might in a manner be termed a second universal medicine, if the conditions above stated are diligently observed."

Pitch

"Pour four pints[6] of cold water over one of pitch, then stir and mix them intimately with a wooden spoon or flat stick, for five to ten minutes, after which let the vessel stand, hermetically sealed, for at least 48 hours, so that the pitch may have time to precipitate. Then pour in all that is clear, having first carefully skimmed it off without shaking the vessel, and fill several bottles with it, which are immediately capped; the pitch that remains has no more virtue, although it can still be used for ordinary purposes."[7]

Good pitch water has an intermediate colour between the colour of the white wine of France and that of Spain; and is equally clear.[8]

Pitch water for external use

"Pour two quarts of boiling water over one quarter of pitch, stir and beat it well with a stick or spoon for a good quarter of an hour, let it stand for ten hours and then pour it off and keep it exactly covered for use. This water may be made weaker or stronger according to need."[9]

---

6 Old measure for wine and other liquids. The pint of Paris was worth a little less than a litre, i.e. 0.931 litres.

7 Monginot, *Conservation de la santé*, Paris, 1635, chap. IX.

8 Berkeley, *Recherches sur les vertus de l'eau de Goudron*, Amsterdam, 1745, pp. 4 and 318, and idem p. 320.

9 Berkeley, *op. cit.*, p. 326.

It is used as a lotion against lithiasis of the kidneys, scabies, ulcers, scrofula and leprosy.

As a drink it is used against the following diseases: smallpox, blood eruptions, ulceration of the intestines, inflammation, gangrene, scurvy, erysipelas, asthma, indigestion, renal lithiasis, dropsy and hysteria.

The best pitch comes from the American pine (*Pinus rigida*).

Spruce trees need dry, high ground and a north wind.

Preparation of hemlock extract

Take fresh hemlock (stems and leaves) in any quantity you wish; squeeze the juice, evaporating it over a very low heat, into an earthen vessel, stirring it from time to time to prevent it from burning; cook it until it has the consistency of a thick extract, add a sufficient quantity of hemlock powder to make a mass, from which you will form two-grain tablets….

> "If, in the absence of the green hemlock, an extract is made from the decoction of the dried plant, this preparation has much less virtue than the former."[10]

The intake of this medicine should be started with very small doses, which may be increased to one and a half *gros*.[11] Immediately after ingestion, prepare a tea, or a calf's broth, or an infusion of elder-flowers.

Dried and chopped hemlock leaves can be used in a sachet which is steeped for a few minutes in boiling water, pressed lightly and applied while hot.

All these preparations are fluxing, resolving and soothing.

The plant called *Cicuta officinarum, Cicuta major, Cicuta vulgaris, Cicutaria major vulgaris, Cicuta vera,* or *Conium maculatum, seu conium steminibus sriatis.*[12]

Theophrastus says that the best hemlock grows in the shade, in cold soils; that of Vienna (Austria) and that around Soissons are more active than those of Paris and Italy.

---

10 Antoni Storck, *Observations nouvelles sur l'usage de la ciguë*, Vienna and Paris, 1762, p. 2, V.

11 Old measure, one gros is one-eighth of an ounce or 28.35 grams.

12 Biological taxonomy, which assigns Latin names to plants and animals has changed with the times. Today (2021), hemlock is called *Conium maculatum* (Editor's note).

Hippocrates,[13] Galen,[14] Mercurialis,[15] Astruc[16] and many other physicians, both of antiquity and of the Middle Ages and Renaissance, used hemlock for internal use as a remedy for tumours, colic and heartburn.

Our fathers also used a quintessence of celandine, lemon balm, valerian, beetroot, saffron and aloe as a general tonic.

Canonical prohibitions

We know that, according to ancient medicine, the astrological conditions at the time of harvest had a great influence on the virtue of the collected herbs; these conditions are indicated in our Dictionary. But lest anyone should be unaware of them, readers should be warned that such practices are forbidden by the Church.

We find in the canons taken from the penitential books of Theodore, Archbishop of Canterbury; of the venerable Bede; of Raban, Archbishop of Mainz; of Halitgarius, Bishop of Cambrai; of the collection published by Luke of Achery; from that of Isaac, Bishop of Langres; d'Eybert, Archbishop of York; from book 19 of the Decree of Burchard; from part 15 of the Decree of Ives, Bishop of Chartres; which all unanimously condemn anyone who observes superstitious signs for planting trees, etc., to do penance for two years on legitimate feasts; he who has collected medicinal herbs with words of incantation shall do penance for twenty days.

J.-F. Bonhomme, apostolic visitor under Gregory XIII, forbids in his decrees (printed at Vercelli in 1579) the gathering of ferns or fern seeds, other herbs or other plants on certain days or nights, having the idea that it would be useless to gather them at another time. "If anyone is guilty of such superstitions, let him be severely punished as it pleases the ordinary of the place."

For the initiate, the magician, the adept, these prohibitions are childish; for the mystic they correspond to a reality, and he obeys them, but for another reason than the simple obedience of the Catholic faithful.

Recollection

The day or eve of St. John's Day is propitious for gathering all kinds of herbs. Moreover, each plant has certain days in the year on which its strength is exalted; the hours of the night are more favourable; the plants may be gathered after hav-

---

13 *De Natura Muliebri*, ed. Linden, vol. 2, p. 279, 71.

14 *De simpl. médicam. Facult.*, Lib. XIII, p. 22, c.; *De temperam*, Lib. III, p. 14 c.; *De Comp. médic. sec. loc.*, Liv. VII, ch. v, p. 184, 4. – *De antidotis*, Liv. II, ch. 13, p. 118, 6.

15 *De morb. mulier*, Liv. IV, ch. 10.

16 *Traité des maladies des femmes*, vol. 2, p. 391.

ing consecrated them with signs and words appropriate to their signature; they are then pulled from the earth or the useful part is cut off with a special knife, indicating the purpose for which they are to be used.

The prohibitions of the Church against these ceremonies have their raison d'être, which is very secret and known to few; suffice it to say, in this respect, that from the truly mystical point of view, in the divine plan, every act of magic is an act of revolt, and must therefore be abstained from.

Hermetic treatment of the plants

Once collected, this treatment is very different from ordinary pharmaceutical manipulation. Its aim is no longer to arrange the physical qualities, the juices of the plant in the most beneficial way, but to release the living force, the essence, the soul or the *balm* of the plant, as the ancient hermetics used to say.

Balsam is the essential oil of the plant; it is neither a vulgar oil, nor salt, nor earth, nor water, but something very subtle, the vehicle of the astral body. It is obtained through fire and not through fermentation (Boerhave).

This balsam is what Paracelsus calls an *arcanum*, that is, a fixed, immortal and in a certain sense incorporeal substance, which changes, restores and preserves bodies; this force is enveloped in a heaven, or *tincture*, which is obtained by reducing the vegetable from its second matter to its crude matter, or, as Paracelsus says, from *cagastrum* to *iliastrum*.

Strictly speaking, the curative power of a plant lies in its spirit; now, in its natural state, the activity of the spirit is hindered and its light obscured by the clothing of matter, it is therefore necessary to destroy these coverings, or at least to transmute them into something pure and fixed; this transmutation is effected by coction, during which a substance capable of absorbing the impurities is added. The choice of this substance must be dictated by the consideration that the taste of a vegetable indicates the hunger which devours it, that is to say, the ideal type towards which it tends; it will be observed of what planetary signature this taste is, and the coction will be begun with a mineral salt of the same planet.

From this coction three things are obtained: a salt, a prime matter and a mercury, that is to say, a fixed water.

> "We burn plants," says St. Thomas in his opuscle, *Lapide Philosophico*, "in the calcining furnace, then we convert this lime into water, distil it and coagulate it; it is then transformed into a stone endowed with more or less great virtues according to the virtues of the plants used and their diversity."

There are three salts or plant powers that are particularly useful for therapeutics.

The first is Jupiterian, with a good smell and a good taste; it is produced internally by a force of divine expansion, and externally by the Sun and Venus. But it is not strong enough to heal by itself; it is the enemy of poisonous igneous life, and determines harmony or a path to sweetness.

The salt of Mars is bitter, igneous and astringent.

Mercury salt is energising and determines healthy reactions.

Jupiter and Venus are the antidotes of the latter two.

The first matter which is then extracted from the plants is nourishing; it is almost always an oil from which the temperament of the sick person draws strength.

Lastly, the mercury of life is regenerative and reviving; it can only be extracted from almost perfect, sweet-tasting plants, which are signed by the Sun, Venus and Jupiter. Rough vegetables do not attack the root of this Mercury; therefore they only act on the four elements, while this Mercury reaches the astral body.

This is a general method of plant preparation; the operator will have to modify it according to the elemental quality of the plant.

The collected plant, cut into small pieces, is put to macerate in hot salt water, one day, in the dark, after having been infused in alcohol, in the sun, for a week. In addition to the alcohol content, the maceration water and the solid residue, dried and even chopped, are kept. Two round-bottom distillation flasks are prepared, by linking them by their necks with great care; they are surrounded with a triple black fleece cloth, after having deposited the residue and the two liquids, and the whole is placed at a constant heat of 39 to 40° C for three weeks; it is necessary to obtain, whatever the plant, a slightly thick, red and fixed liquor; although all the gases, liquids and solids obtained have special qualities.

Cure

In general, it is best to use the salts of Mars and Mercury, as the most active, uniting them by Venus and Jupiter, so that they find as it were to extinguish the fire of their anger; when this is accomplished, the cure is done, that is to say, harmony is restored; and there is nothing more to do than to give a little sunlight to set everything in motion again.

The physician should know that good plants can be spoilt by a bad look, especially from Saturn and Mars, and that poisonous plants can be made beneficial by the Sun, Venus or Jupiter.

Every ailment should be cured by its like; not to give a ♀ plant for a ♄ disease; but to administer an herb where it has improved by the use of art the wrath of Mars by Jupiter and Venus; the hotter a plant is, the better it is, provided its wrath has been transmuted into love, for if the poison falls into the property of Mercury, death comes soon.

Primum ens melissae, according to Paracelsus

Take half a litre of carbonate of potassium and expose it to the air until it dissolves; filter the liquid and put into it as many leaves of lemon balm as you can,[17] so that all are immersed in the liquid. Keep in a closed place, over a gentle fire for 21 hours; decant; pour over the pure liquid a layer of alcohol one or two inches thick, and leave it there for two days, or until the alcohol becomes a beautiful green colour; this alcohol should be collected, as it is good for use, and replaced by another alcohol until all the colouring matter has been absorbed; the alcohol will then be distilled and evaporated to a syrupy consistency.

Both the alcohol and the alkali must be highly concentrated.

Counter-poison

One of the most active counter poisons against vegetable poisons is the following composition:

Tartar and alcohol are heated together at a moderate, but constant temperature, and distil in the retort a red oil, endowed with special properties. This oil, digested four times in succession, gives the indicated counter-poison.

---

17 Paracelsus called lemon balm (*Melissa officinalis*) the elixir of life, and combined it with carbonate of potassium, as here indicated, in a mixture known as *Primum Ens Melissae.*

§ III. – Magic

Since Magic is, first and foremost, a practical art, when a creature is studied from this point of view, it is the individuality, the person that must be taken care of. All the magic of the plant kingdom thus lies in the knowledge of the *spirits* of the plants. They are the spirits of plants, known in antiquity as *dryads, hamadryads, silvanus* and *fauns*; they are the *Dusii* of St. Augustine, the fairies of the Middle Ages, the *Doire Oigh* of the Welsh, the *Grove Maidens* of the Irish. Paracelsus calls *sylvan* those who inhabit the forests, and *nymphs* those of the aquatic plants.

To see the spirits of the forests

After the usual purifications, go to the forest early in the morning, and find a place where the trees are thick enough to hide the sky completely. Then sit down, keep your eyelids half closed, but your eyes fixed, and mentally invoke the *silvanus*, that is, the spirits of the forest, by whatever name you call them; you will surely see them appear, especially if you offer them water, or wheat, and if you persist for several days. (II, J. Bjerregard)

These beings belong to the class of what occultism calls elementals; they are inhabitants of the astral who aspire to elevate themselves to the human condition; they are endowed with a certain instinctive intelligence, and change form at the same time as the material being to which they are united. They are those whom the ancient Rosicrucians used in their miraculous healings, for they are servants, and obey quite naturally the commands of the spiritual man.

Their power is quite great on the material plane because they dwell on the boundary of that plane and the astral plane; they can produce amazing healings or visions; just as the elementals of the mineral kingdom produce, when properly directed, all alchemical phenomena, and those of the animal kingdom, the great majority of spiritual manifestations.

Religious magic

Plant symbolism is highly developed in the sacred books of ancient religions. We need only recall here the tree of the knowledge of good and evil and the tree of life in Eden: symbols of the two methods which Adam could follow to fulfil his mission; the tree of the Sephiroth of the Kabalah; the Aswatta or sacred fig tree, symbol of total knowledge; the Haoma of the Mazdeans, through which Zoroaster represented the blood and nervous system of man and of the Universe; the Zampoun of Tibet; the Yggradsil, the Oak of Pherecydes and of the ancient Celts.

All these symbols have many different meanings; which we will not mention here, lest we stray too far from our subject, which is concerned with mental development. All religious legends represent to us the adepts, acquiring omniscience under a tree; only Christ, who is, among other things, science itself, is not represented under this symbolism; the reason for this is quite hidden; it has to do with the creature's own definition, or, if one prefers, with the double use he can make of his free will. Thus the whole religious symbolism comprises two trees; the Kabbalistic or Egyptian tradition alone indicates them, because it was to be crowned by the descent of the Son of God; the other traditions, being the heritage of disintegrating races, give to the outer world only the Tree of Science.

In naturalistic initiations, the Tree of Science is nothing other than the image of the inner man; its trunk is the spinal cord, its branches are the 72,000 nerves known to the Hindu yogis, it has seven flowers, which are the seven centres of the astral body; its leaves are the double respiratory apparatus hidden in the lungs; its roots are the genital pole and the legs; its sap is the cosmic electricity which runs through the nerves and takes shape from the cerebral ether to the spermatic earth.

The word *Yoga* is the Sanskrit synonym for the word religion; both mean the link that unites man with the Universe and with God; its process is the same as that by which a seed takes from a black earth and informs the molecules that it will form a fragrant flower. According to the practitioner's ideal, *Yoga* transmutes the impure molecules of the physical body into fixed and unchanging molecules, the lower passions into pure enthusiasm, intellectual ignorance into the light of truth. This is why the Masters of *Yoga* are depicted sitting under a sacred tree.

Natural magic

The various traditions teach many uses of occult plant forces. Plants can be used as a whole or taking only one of its parts.

The first method relates to this type of pact, widely used among the natives of Central America, New Guinea, New Zealand, India and Germany, whereby the destiny of a newborn child is linked to that of a particular tree. A very close relationship develops between these two creatures; the child benefits from the vigour of the tree, but if the tree is injured, the child suffers and dies.

Bewitched trees

There is no village in India that does not have its own haunted tree, whose genius is worshipped by the people of the lower classes.

Hellenic traditions also said that every forest has its genie and every tree its nymph.

It is not uncommon to see, in the Nilgiris,[18] a large tree decorated with figures drawn in vermilion, and having at its base three stones painted red, such trees are places of sacrifice and worship, where animal remains or braids of hair are offered by the sick or possessed.[19] The guardian spirits of these trees are called *Mounispourams* by the natives; they are generally beneficent, but their power is limited to a single object.

The natives usually consecrate one of their children to these genii, for a period of seven years or more, at the end of which time a great sacrifice is offered, and the child's hair is hung on the tree.

Such trees belong chiefly to the oak family; sometimes wild cinnamon and eugenia are found in the same case (*Theosophist*, November 1894.).

Philtres

The word "philtres" designates any kinds of drinks that take into their composition substances magically prepared for the occult attainment of a certain result. The three kingdoms of nature provide many materials for these preparations; we shall deal only with the substances provided by the vegetable kingdom.

Ointments, electuaries, pomades, salves, collyrium, or magic drinks, almost all from come from the realm of black magic. Their number is very great and can be increased indefinitely by an ingenious mind. Thus, the Chinese Taoist priests use only thirteen plants, animal and mineral substances for all purposes of medicine, psychology and magic, but they know how to extract a great number of combinations.

---

18 The Nilgiris, or *Blue Mountains*, are a mountain range situated in southern India.

19 The Polish *plique* is cured in particular in this way. The word *plique* is a medical term, referring to a disease observed especially in Poland and characterised by the intertwining and clumping of hair.

These preparations can be used on oneself or on others. They all act on the astral body, on one of its three great centres: the instinctive, the passionate and the mental.

In the first case, they produce health, disease and all possible physiological phenomena. In the second, they produce love, hatred and other passions. In the third, they produce somnambulism, clairvoyance, clairaudience or even phenomena of a higher order.

The traditional folklore, the stories of the Sabbaths, the tales that everyone has heard of poisonings and murders at a distance, of beasts or of people, can be explained by the action of these magical substances acting on the instinctual centre. The same applies to the stories of love philtres, but the use of plants to provoke psychic phenomena is less well known; this art is still practised today in the East, in most Buddhist monasteries, among the Chinese Taoists, the Tibetan Lamas, the Tantrics of Bhutan, the shamans of Turkestan and certain Muslim dervish brotherhoods; not to mention the mechanical use made of it by almost all the savage tribes of the various continents.

Hashish and opium are two of the best known of the mentally active herbal substances; but no one in the West knows how to handle them scientifically unless he has been initiated into their use in the Far East. The stories of Quincey or Baudelaire, whatever their artistic merit and sincerity, do not give rise to the possibilities of such adjuvants. All we can say is that the use of these drugs can only lead to intellectual ecstasy if the subject has known, beforehand, without excitement and by force of will alone, to master his mental forces and become capable of governing the association of ideas; and this is no easy task. – Otherwise, if a hashish-consumer has not fixed his mind, he sets out on an adventure, in a rudderless ship, on an ocean more terrible than the Indian Sea with its cyclones; and he may return from it with madness as his companion, or even not return at all.

Ragon, the great modern interpreter of Freemasonry, set forth in one of his works, certain novel experiments; he took discs of different colours, coated them with the juice of various plants, and caused magnetised subjects to behold them; here are the results of these experiments. (See Table in next page.)

We will not advise anyone to repeat these experiments; their clearest result is to disturb the nervous system of the unfortunate subjects, under the fallacious pretext of immediate scientific utility.

We also condemn all practices of natural and psychic magic, except in cases of therapy. The satisfaction of love or hatred, the vain acquisition of intellectual knowledge, are not things important enough to prevent the exercise of free will and to hinder the normal development of the laws of the Universe. Only one thing is necessary: to love God and one's neighbour; all else is vain and perishable.

Discs	Plants	Effects produced
1. Violet	Henbane (*Hyoscyamus niger*) Belladonna (*Atropa belladonna*) Stramonium (*Datura stramonium*) Marijuana (*Cannabis indica*) Strychnine (*Strychnos nux-vomica*)	Continuous movement of arms and legs; desire to touch something or to walk on any object; screaming, barking, imitation of dogs; desire to bite and hit someone with a knife; complete drunkenness; appearances of all kinds of happiness; everything he desires, he possesses in illusion. He remembers everything that happened and everything he saw.
2. Indigo	Black pepper (*Piper nigrum*) Sabadilla (*Schoenocaulon officinale*)	Febrile excitement; weakness in abdominal extremities. Subject kneels and wants to recite a prayer, but he cannot remember a single one. Loss of sight, though he walks with ease; banging against walls; trembling of eyelids; eyes eventually close; deep sleep (we can only wake him by pouring water on his face).
3. Blue	Java pepper (*Piper cubeba*) Camphor tree (*Cinnamomum camphora*) Asafoetida (*Ferula assafoetida*) Hemlock (*Conium maculatum*)	General excitement, convulsive movement; desire to sleep; loss of all reasoning; drowsiness, despondency.
4. Green	*Pseu. angust.* *Lact. vir.* *Atr. mand.*	Profound tears; plays with hands like a child; desire to run; pretends to walk faster than a horse. Contractions of all muscles of body; wants to say good-bye, as if he would die; general numbness; lethargy.
5. Yellow	Strychnine (*Strychnos nux-vomica*) Opium (*Papaver somniferum*) St Ignatius faba bean (*Strychnos ignatii*) Lettuce (*Lactuca sativa*) White hellebore (*Lactuca sativa*) White hellebore (*Veratrum album*) Asparagus (*Asparagus officinalis*)	Balancing of the head; general drowsiness, sleepiness (on opening the eyelids, the presence of the yellow disc gives him a great fury, though he cannot explain its cause, the other colours have no effect on him). Voluptuous dreams, shivering and extreme pallor; despondency; new sleep; state of magnetisation during which he can walk, stroll and see perfectly, although his eyelids are completely closed; he answers questions about different things he does not know (when he wakes up he has no memory of what he said, or what happened).
6. Orange	Opium salt Valerian (*Valeriana officinalis*) Tobacco (*Nicotiana tabacum*) *Convul. jal.*	Great joy; numbness of upper and lower limbs; sleepiness (on opening the eyelids and presenting him with the orange disc, he feels a great desire to laugh, interrupted by moral suffering which he cannot explain); tears, tendency to great lucidity.
7. Red	Plum (*Prunus domestica*) Lavender (*Lavandula angustifolia*) Digitalis (*Digitalis purpurea*)	Fear, fear of people in hiding. Acute seizure. May take from 2.5 hours to 4–5 hours to recover.

Ointment of the Sorcerers

Here is some information that we extract, as a curiosity, from a very little known book that we had the good fortune to consult in the library of our dear departed master, Stanislas de Guaita.

"Among all the medicinal herbs that the Devil uses to disturb the senses of his slaves, the following seem to have the first rank, they are those that have the virtue of causing deep sleep; the others only cause slight or no sleep, but disturb and deceive the senses, with various figures and representations, both in waking and sleeping, as *the root of belladonna, the furious blackberry herb, the blood of bats, the hoopoe, aconite, wild celery, tallow, sweet flag, parsley, poplar leaves, opium, henbane, hemlock, different poppy species, tares* and *synochytides*, which shows the shadows of hell, i.e. evil spirits; as well as, on the other hand, the anacytid, which makes the images of the Holy Angels appear". [20]

Nynauld recognises three types of ointments in the devilish pharmacopoeia. The first one, which only gives dreams, consists of fat, wild celery, aconite, potentilla, blackberry herb and soot.

By the virtue of the ointments of the second type, "the Devil persuades the witches, after having anointed their bodies, to be able, by putting a broom or a stick between their legs, to ride in the air, and to go to their Synagogues with incredible speed, passing through the chimney… It is to be remarked that in the composition of this ointment no simple narcotic herbs are used, but only those which have the virtue of disturbing the senses by alienating them, such as *wine taken inordinately, cat's brains, belladonna,* and other things which I will keep silent, lest I should give the malefactors an opportunity of doing mischief."[21]

The third ointment is given by the devil to witches, "persuading them that after being anointed with it, they will be truly transformed into beasts, and thus be able to run through the fields". It includes parts of the body of a toad, a snake, a hedgehog, a fox, human blood, certain herbs and roots, of which Nynauld does not indicate the dosage [22]

The counsellor of Eckartshausen, who lived at the end of the eighteenth century,[23] gives the following formula for having apparitions: pellets composed of hemlock, henbane, saffron, aloes, opium, mandrake, poppy, asafoetida, and parsley; all dried and burnt.

---

20 Nynauld. *Licanthropie*, chap. II.

21 I will imitate the prudent reserve of Dr. de Nynauld, in not mentioning the quantities of the malignant composition, nor the manner of its preparation.

22 *Ob Cit.,* chap. III.

23 *Aufschlüsse zur Magie.*

Against evil spirits, he indicates sulphur, asafoetida, castoreum, hypericum and vinegar.

Nynauld, already quoted, indicates in chapter VII of his book the following perfumery formulas:

To see strange things: heather root, hemlock juice, henbane juice and black poppy seeds.

To see future things: flax seeds and psellium, violet roots and wild celery.

To ward off evil spirits: calamint, peony, mint and castor.

If you burn dry gall, thyme, rose, aloe wood, and pour water over it, the house will seem full of water; or of blood if you pour blood over it; if you pour earth, the ground will tremble.

§ IV. – AGRONOMY

Cultivation of plants

There is a magical agriculture whose precepts and *modus operandi* have also been lost. The foundation of this art consists in sowing the seed in the exact matrix that complements it. Just as, in the regime of mysticism, the man who has found his heavenly type, becomes by this fact powerful in deeds and words, so the seed sown in its own soil, attains its generic perfection.

Sowing is done under the auspices of *Saturn*; the Gauls called *sat*, the seed, and *satur* the sower; to sow is to put something in darkness, in depth and in isolation.

Darkness provokes light, and the formless mass of rotting cotyledons calls forth the radiant flower or the majestic tree.

Let us see what happens to the great majority of seedlings, that is to say, when the soil does not correspond in all respects to the germ entrusted to it. We have seen that the subterranean development of the latter takes place at the expense of the *Salt, Sulphur* and *Mercury* of the earth; the sun is there as the universal dispenser of life; but its invisible vital rays are only assimilable for a seed if they are presented to it qualified in complementary correspondence with it. If, therefore, the soil in which the seed lies does not satisfy these conditions, the *Entity* of the germ spreads out rootlets, exhausting its strength, seeking around it what it needs; then the root grows dry and gnarled, as does the stem: the *Salt, Sulphur* and *Mercury* consume themselves and consume without result the solar life which comes to them, preventing it from being assimilated.

Art can remedy this fundamental disadvantage in two ways: by carefully choosing the right soil for the germ that will fertilise it, or, if the plant has already germinated, by giving it a vital stimulant.

In the first case, it is necessary to know thoroughly the proportion in which *Salt, Sulphur* and *Mercury* participate in the composition of the soil and the seed, or the chemical composition of both.

In the second case, during the preparation of the stone, especially by the dry method, various deposit liquors are produced, which work very well as medicine for weak plants.

This will be discussed later in the next topic: *Magical Growth of Plants.*

Besides the relation of the plant to the soil which nourishes it physically, there is the choice of its society; some plants thrive by living side by side with others, and wither if their neighbours dislike them; it is here a question of signatures, as will be seen by the following examples, and much more, by daily experience.

The olive tree is a friend of the vine and stays away from the cabbage.

The buttercup is a friend of the water lily.

The rue is friendly to the fig tree, etc.

Finally, external agents, especially light, also have their influence on plant life. The blue ray of the spectrum activates vegetation, and the yellow ray slows it down. Camille Flammarion has made conclusive experiments on this point.

Plant collection

Astrological doctrine teaches that plants should be gathered at certain planetary hours, or better still at the time of the conjunctions of the favourable planets that signify them, and when the evil stars are in exile. The *Little Dictionary of Botany* indicates the different cases which may occur.

§ V. – MAGICAL GROWTH OF PLANTS

Dr. Carl de Prel[24] quoted Simon the Magician[25] as saying: "At my gesture, the earth is covered with vegetation, and the trees grow… I can make the ephebes grow beards… More than once, I have made bushes grow out of the earth in an instant".

Christophe Langhans tells the following story of his travels:[26]

"A fakir asked for an apple of *Sina*; he split it, took out a seed and buried it in the earth, having moistened it a little beforehand; he covered the place with a small basket, put a handful of tobacco in his mouth and stuck a waxed thread under his lip, stuck the slimy tobacco from his mouth on this thread, restarting the operation after the thread was covered for the first time. He then lifted the basket and showed us that in half an hour a plant had grown out of the ground. He soon covered the plant, made a few contortions, and then removed the basket at the bottom of which was the plant, which bore fragrant flowers; his companions made a few more contortions, after which fruit was seen on the tree. To ripen them, he began again to coat his thread with tobacco, and, fifteen minutes later, presented us with five very beautiful and ripe apples; I tasted them, found them resembling natural fruits; the commissary kept one of them; but the fakir plucked the tree himself and put it in water."

Here is another testimony from a modern traveller:

"On the verandah of one of the early hotels on the main street, my eyes were fixed on the movements of a group of jugglers squatting on the ground. All their clothing consisted of the usual strip of calico wrapped round their loins, so that they could not help themselves to it for their exercises. These were the most skilful people I had ever seen…

---

24 *Forciertes Pflanzenvachstum*. Sphinx, March 1889.
25 Gorres, *La mystique chrétienne*, III, p. 108.
26 *Neue ostindische Reise*, 1705.

> "One of them put a nut on the ground, covered it with two pieces of cloth, which he lifted several times, to put the idea of deception out of our minds.
>
> "The nut first cracked open, grew little by little, till in about ten minutes it became a real small bush, with leaves and roots."[27]

Similar facts have been observed in Europe. In 1715, a physician named Agricola made the following experiments at Ratisbon in the presence of Count Wratislaus:

1. He made twelve lemons grow into lemon trees with roots, branches and fruit.

2. At the same time he did the same with apples, peaches and apricots, which he grew to a height of four and five feet.

3. To complete the remainder of the hour devoted to these experiments, he brought 15 almonds in the form of seedlings, which then continued their normal development.[28]

Finally, we will conclude these wonderful accounts with one still more wonderful, in which the phenomenon is produced by a ghost;[29] it is always from the work of Dr. du Prel that we borrow the details; the celebrated scientist heard them confirmed by an eye-witness.

In a spiritualist circle, an English medium, Miss d'Espérance, obtained the materialisation of a spirit who called herself Yolande. – During one of her materialisations, the ghost asked for a bottle, water and sand, and she put all this into the bottle which she placed on the floor, describing around it circular passes; seeds of *Ixora crocata* and *Anthurium Schezerianum*; she covered the artefact with a piece of white cloth, and retired to the black cabinet from which she had materialised. Instantly we saw the cloth lifted up in the bottle, and Yolande showed us a plant with green leaves, roots and buds; the bottle was placed back on the ground, and the ghost entered the black cabinet, and four or five minutes passed, after which the whole audience, which included not less than twenty persons, could examine at leisure the two small plants, which were six inches high and covered with fresh and bright flowers. Similar accounts can be found in the writings of Tavernier (*Voyage en turquie*) and du Potet (*Journal du magnétisme*, XVI, 14), Gouguenot des Mousseaux (*Les hauts phénomènes de la magie*, p. 230) and of Gorres (III, 554).

---

27 J. Hingston, *The Australian Abroad*, London, 1880.

28 Francus de Frankenau, *De Palingenesia*, p. 140.

29 *Herald of Progress*, September 3, 1880, Hellenbach, *Magie der Zahlen*, p. 155.

The well–known experiences of Louis Jacolliot,[30] whose works are widely distributed, confirm these ancient accounts.

Advanced philosophers are not theoretically opposed to these experiments.

"We know –says Edouard von Hartmann–, that the physiological functions of plant life can be powerfully excited by rays of bright light, either by electricity or by chemical adjuvants; that even in man, a child of four years of age can attain the development of a subject of thirty years, and that certain seeds, which grow naturally fast, can be artificially accelerated in their maturation. According to this, it is reasonable to suppose that the mediumistic force may operate in a similar way."[31]

Dr. du Prel, from whom we have borrowed all these quotations, constructs a very interesting theory as follows.

The organic life of man, as well as his intellectual life, offer an example of the action of an accelerating power analogous to that which we see at work in plants. Our author recalls the mention he made in another work[32] of the alteration of time in certain dream phenomena, during which pictures pass before our eyes, apparently for hours, but in reality their parade lasts only a few seconds.

Man, in the womb, in nine months, goes through a biological process which, in external nature, lasts millions of years.[33] Why should it be impossible for an exercised will to build around a vegetable or animal, or even mineral *mind*, an invisible matter which provides this *mind* with a much more dynamic, i.e. more spiritual, nourishment?… this is what the fakir does, as Dr. Papus says, in his treatise on practical magic (*Magie pratique*), who develops the seed with his vital force by laying his hand on it. His soul is concentrated in a certain focus of his astral body called in Sanskrit, the *Swadishtana Tchakra*, and it is the forces of vegetative life that nourish and develop the phenomenon.

Instead of borrowing the materials of his invisible food from a human organism, one can borrow them from Nature, and this is what constitutes the alchemical process of which we show two formulae:

–Take one ounce of *Marte* and one ounce of *Venus*; macerate at 75° C in a thick distillation ball; a green or red *caput mortuum*[34] and a greenish dissolving

---

30 *Le Spiritisme dans le Monde*, pp. 309–314.

31 *Der Spiritismus*, 53, note.

32 *La Philosophie de la Mystique*. See also on this subject, *Les Rêves et les moyens de les diriger*; we note also how certain drowned persons, at the moment of their death, have remembered their whole life.

33 Cf. *Anthropogeny*. Haceckel.

34 Caput mortuum is a Latin expression whose literal meaning is "dead head" or "remains", used in alchemy.

liquor will be deposited. Distil to dryness, cohobate[35] five or six times so that nothing is left in the retort. Evaporation will give a fixed red salt. If the seeds are infused in water where a little of this salt has been put, these seeds will grow faster; their will have a golden glow and the fruits will be better.

Drinking gold

Here is one of the many formulas used to make this liquor:

Heat to 400 °C a quantity of magisterium[36] of sulphur. Gelatinous at first, the mass is melted again, distilled, and finally leaves a residue. This residue is collected and mixed intimately with a salt that can fix it; the mixture is distilled with a strong fire, the *caput mortuum* is sieved out; and this operation is repeated until the distillation only produces insipid water.

Treated with pure alcohol (such as salt of tartar, see *Counter-poison*, in p. 52), the result is an oil and water which must be decanted. This water dissolves the gold salt; when saturated with metal, it is good for watering diseased vines, stunted fruit trees, etc.

---

35 *Cohobate* is a pharmacist's term. To distil a liquor several times in succession over its residue, or better still over new substances, so that it takes on more volatile principles.

36 Pharmacy term. Name given to generally mineral compounds to which superior virtues were supposed, which were kept prepared in pharmacies, the preparation of which was often secret, and which were so called because they were magisterial things, magisterial preparations.

§ VI. – Palingenesis

At the present day, we deal little with the mysterious problems of the biology of the three lower kingdoms of Nature; the more intuitive of our contemporaries feel that there is something else behind the chemistry, behind the botany, and behind the official zoology. This something, the great initiates of all times have known, and have even let it shine out into the world. If Alchemy is famous in the history of the scientific development of our West, Occult Botany is much less known and Occult Zoology is not known at all. All three exist, however, as successive developments of a single notion: earthly life.

For each one of the three kingdoms of this Life, we can reconstruct the Art and Science which were dedicated to them in the ancient Temples of Wisdom; but this is not the place to develop such seductive hypotheses; we shall only seek in these vanished syntheses the materials strictly necessary to construct the theory of the subject we are developing.

Between the material and the spiritual world there is an intermediary, which is the astral world; this astral world, which is repeated throughout the three kingdoms of Nature, is called, according to Paracelsus, the *Leffas*[37] for the plants, and combined with their vital force, it constitutes the *Ens primum*, which possesses the highest curative virtues; this is the subject of Palingenesis.

As we can see, this art is threefold, consisting of reviving the soul, i.e. simply the ghost of the plant; or reviving the body and soul of the plant; or finally, creating it with materials borrowed from the mineral kingdom. – We shall give some palingenetic recipes which all refer to the first work; nothing has ever been written about the physical resurrection and creation of plants.

> "A certain Polonois knew how to enclose the ghosts of plants in their vials; so, whenever he wished, he would make a plant appear in an empty vial. Each vessel contained its own plant: at the bottom was a little earth, like ashes. It was sealed with the seal of Hermes. When he wanted to expose

---

37 Astral bodies of plants. They can be made visible from the ashes of the plants after they have been burnt.

it to view, he would gently heat the bottom of the container. The penetrating heat caused the stem, branches, leaves and flowers to emerge from the bosom of the matter, according to the nature of the plant whose soul he had enclosed; the plant appeared complete before the eyes of the spectators, as long as he applied the exciting heat to it."[38]

It is invariably on the morphic pattern of the plant, on its *sidereal body* or potential, substrate of visible matter (itself reduced to the state of *caput mortuum*), that the vegetable phantom takes shape, in ephemeral objectification in the first case; and in the other, it presides, in vegetative mode, over the molecular grouping of the nascent crystal.

In the *Grand Livre de la nature* (Great Book of Nature), published in the last century thanks to the dedication of a chapter of the Rosicrucians, we find all the phases of the spagyric operation necessary to obtain the vegetable phoenix. This is the case prepared for the proof of palingenesis, to which the author refers with this metaphor. As for the essential manipulations, we will take note of the prescription with reservations, trying to summarise the details of the meticulous prescriptions formulated from page 15 to page 19.

"1° Four pounds of very ripe seeds of the plant whose soul it is desired to liberate, must be carefully crushed, then this paste must be preserved at the bottom of a very transparent and clear container.

"2° One evening, when the atmosphere is pure and the sky is serene, expose the product to the humidity of the night, so that it may be impregnated with the invigorating virtue that is in the dew.

"3° and 4° Eight pints of this dew must be collected and filtered, but before sunrise, which would suck out the most precious part, which is extremely volatile;

"5° The filtered liquor is then distilled: from the residue or lees one must know how to extract a salt 'very curious and very pleasant to see'.

"6° The seeds are watered with the product of the distillation, which is saturated with the salt in question. The container is then buried in horse manure and hermetically sealed with borax and crushed glass.

"7° At the end of a month, 'the seed will have turned into jelly; the spirit will be like a skin of various colours which will float over all the matter'. Between the skin and the slimy substance at the bottom there is a kind of greenish dew which represents a harvest.[39]

---

38 Guy de La Brosse, *De la nature, vertu et utilité des plantes*, etc. 1644; cit. p. Guaita, *Clé de la magie noire*.

39 *Le Grand Livre de la Nature ou l'Apocalypse philosophique et hermétique*, etc., seen by a Society of unknown philosophers and published by D.... – In the South and at the printing house of the *Vérité* (1790), pp. 17–18.

"8º At this point of fermentation, the mixture must be exposed, in its exactly closed flask, by day to the burning sun, by night to the lunar irradiation. During rainy periods, the container is kept in a dry and warm place until the good weather returns. – It takes several months, often a year, for the operation to be perfect. On the one hand, the material blisters and doubles its volume; on the other hand, the film disappears… This is a sure sign of success.

"9º The material, in its final phase of development, must have a powdery appearance and a blue colour.

"…It is from this powder that the trunk, branches and leaves of the plant rise when the container is exposed to gentle heat. This is how the vegetable Phoenix is made.

"The palingenesis of vegetables would be only an object of amusement, if this operation did not aim at greater and more useful ones. Chemistry can, by its art, revive other bodies; it destroys them with fire and then restores them to their original form. The transmutation of metals and the Philosopher's Stone are a continuation of metallic palingenesis.

"We do with animals what we do with plants; but such is the strength of my commitments, that I cannot explain this openly.[40]

"The most marvellous degree of palingenesis is the art of practising on the remains of animals.

"What a delight it is to enjoy the pleasure of perpetuating the shadow of a friend, when he is gone. Artemisia swallowed the ashes of *Mausolus*; she did not know, alas, the secret of cheating her grief."[41]

Can one conceive the value of this rapid indication? The homogeneity of Universal Nature enables man to infer by analogy, and if he has reasoned correctly, experience always confirms his inductions. Now, what occurs in the vegetable kingdom must occur in parallel in the kingdoms below and above it; it is to justify, in the one, the transmutation of metals; in the other, the posthumous rebirth of abolished forms.

In spite of all the enthusiasm which such lofty prospects may excite, let it be said at once that the practice of palingenesis is not free from all moral defects, and that sooner or later it makes its adherents pay dearly for its favours.

---

40 This study (says the author further on) is that of the unknown philosophers. It is from them that I have obtained the truths which I record in this book (p. 22).

41 *Le Grand Livre de la Nature*, pp. 18–19.

§ VII. – Historical and Practical Palingenesis

By Karl Kiesewtter

Inspired by the example given by Dr. Du Prel in his articles on Accelerated Vegetation and the Phoenix of Plants,[42] we believe that it will not fail to be of interest to our readers to have an overview both of the history of the theories and experiments of palingenesis, and of the practices applied. Then, through their personal experiences, which require care for many details, it is true, but are not costly, they may, we say, be able to realise the value or lack of value of the object we are dealing with. I am all the more able to inform you in this respect because, for many years now, I have been able to collect instructions on this question, most of which are difficult to discover and have never been published before, and because, on the other hand, I have taken care to discard everything that the previous era confused with palingenesis, for example, the phenomena of *generatio alquivoqua*, arboreal metallic precipitates and crystallisation, among which is the palingenesis of nettles in the frozen lye of their salt, mentioned by Joseph Duchesne (under his Latin name, *Quercetanus*, 154-10), physician to Henry IV of France.[43]

We shall distinguish two types of palingenesis.

1. The palingenesis of shadows, which has for its object the production of the astral body, whether vegetable or animal.

2. The palingenesis of bodies, which involves the acceleration of plant's functions (forced vegetation) and at the same time aims to reconstitute the destroyed organised bodies. In its ultimate consequences, this enters into the domain of the *Homunculus*, this chemical evocation of the

---

42 Extracted from *l'Initiation*, April 1896.
43 See volume VII of *Sphinx*, especially the fascicle of April 1889.

human being, the point where the extremes of mysticism and materialism come into contact.

Ovid already speaks in advance in exact terms of forced vegetation when he says of his Medea.[44]

> "Of all these substances and a thousand others that cannot be named, compose the filter for the dying old man; then, with an olive branch long since withered and unleafed, mix them together and stir them from the bottom to the surface. But now the old branch, stirred in the boiling bronze, begins to green, and is soon covered with juice. Where the fire makes the foam gush out of the vase and fall to the earth from the burning drops, grass and spring flowers bloom amidst the copious grasses."

Alchemists repeatedly set up palingenetic experiments. Abu Bekre al Rhali (nicknamed Rhasés, who died in 942) and Albertus the Great, in particular, had to deal with our subject.[45] Moreover, the latter goes so far as to affirm that he discovered the Homunculi,[46] and in the Œuvre végétal of Isaac Hollandus[47] there are remarks on palingenesis.

It is only in Paracelsus that we find more detailed indications on the two species of palingenesis. On the palingenesis of shadows he expresses himself in these terms:[48]

> "From this it follows that a force *primi entis* (primordial entity) is enclosed in a phial and brought to this point, in order to give birth in this same phial to a form of the same plant and this without the aid of an earth; and, when this plant has reached the end of its growth, what it has produced is not a *corpus* (body), for the first reason, it has not had a *liquidum terrae*, and its layer is something which has existence only for the eye, something which the finger returns to the state of juice; it is only a smoke which affects the form of a substance, but which offers no hold, that is to say, something immaterial, incapable of impressing the sense of touch."

---

44 See volume VII of *Sphinx*, 40, p. 197. Moreover, the palingenesis of the plants that had been burned to extract the potash could be seen in the frost-covered windowpanes. Compare Eckartshausen, *Eclaircissements sur la magie*, II, p. 3. Whoever wants to get an idea of all that was understood by palingenesis and the role of the imagination in what was seen, has only to read and re-read Jean Otto von Helbig's *Physica curiosa* (Sonderhausen, 1700, in-8). Oettinger's melissa leaf could also be placed among the products of his imagination.

45 Campanelle, *De sensu rerum et magia*. 1620, in-4.

46 Printed several times.

47 *Archidoxorum libri* X, 1. I.

48 *Métamorphoses*, 32, 275–284.

Paracelsus does not give instructions on the palingenesis of shadows, but on that of bodies, when he says:[49]

> "Take a bird that has just been born, enclose it hermetically[50] in a flask and reduce it to ashes over a suitable fire. Then immerse the whole vessel with the ashes of the incinerated bird in horse dung and leave it there until a viscous substance (product of the ashes and empyreumatic oils) is formed; put this substance in an eggshell, close it with the greatest care and incinerate it in the usual manner: you will then see the previously incinerated bird reappear".

Count Kenelm Digby (1603-1665) claims to have reconstituted burnt crayfish in the same way,[51] and Paracelsus wanted to extend this method of palpation to all species of animals. His contemporary, Agrippa of Nettesheim, seems to have known this process, since he says:[52]

> "There is an artifice by which, in an egg placed under a brooding hen, a human figure is created, such as I have seen and am able to execute myself. The magicians attribute to such a figure marvellous powers and call it the true mandrake."[53]

We shall return to this later.

Following the example of their master, the Paracelsians occupied themselves with palingenesis and wrote much about it. Let us cite among them Gaston de Claves (*Clavœus*),[54] *Quercetanus*,[55] Pierre Borreli,[56] Nicolas Béguin,[57] Otto Tachenius,[58] Daniel Sennert,[59] A.– F. Pezold,[60] Kenelm Digby,[61] David van der Becke[62] and William Maxwell.[63] The work of the rector of Hindelberg, Franck von

---

49 Eckartshausen, *Éclaircissements sur la magie*, II, p. 390. I have not had occasion to study closely Jammy's great edition of the works of Albertus Magnus; however, I will communicate below a manuscript instruction attributed to him, concerning palingenesis.

50 *De natura rerum.*

51 I.e. sheltered from air and direct contact with fire.

52 Maurer, *Amphitheatrum magiae universae.*

53 *De Occulta Philosophia*, L. I, ch. XXXVI.

54 *Philosophia chemi.*, Genr. and Lugd. Bat. 1612.

55 *Defensio contra anonymum.*

56 *Historiarum medico-physicarum centurum*, IV, Francof. 1670, in-8.

57 *Tyrocinium chymicium*, Paris, 1600, in-8.

58 *Hippocrates chymicus*, Yanet, 1666, in-12.

59 *Opera omnia*, Lugd. 1650, in-folio; t.III, p.706 and 750.

60 *Ephem. natur. curios. centur.*, VII, obs. 12.

61 *Dissertatio de plantarum vegetatione.*

62 *Experimenta et meditationes circa naturalium rerum principia*, Hambourg, 1683 in-8.

63 *Medicina magnetica.*

Frankenau, is far from exhausting the material and, from the experimental point of view, is mainly based on the indications, in fact concordant, of Borelli, Tachenius and Van der Becke. As far as I know, the latest testimony to palingenetic practice comes from Eckartshausen, who says:[64] "Two of our friends saw actual experiments, instituted in different ways; they witnessed the manipulations and carried them out themselves. One revived a buttercup and the other a rose; they also made experiments on animals which were successful. And it is according to their principles and their method that I also want to work".

William Maxwell, the 17th century Gustave Joeger, speaks of palingenesis in several places in his works. But, unfortunately, he does so in the manner of his master Fludd, that is to say, in a confused and foolishly mysterious way. On the palingenesis of shadows, in the first place, he expresses himself in these terms:[65]

> "Take a sufficient quantity of rose leaves, dry them in the fire, and finally blow them with the bellows until they are reduced to a very white ash (this result may be obtained by simple combustion, in a crucible set red, of dried rose leaves). Then extract the salt under running water and put it into a kolatorium (one of those useless devices of the old chemistry; any bottle covered with emery cloth will do the same service), the openings of which you have sealed as well as possible; leave this kolatorium on the fire for three months (that is, of course, exposed to the gentle heat of digestion), then bury it in manure (as mentioned above) and leave it there for three months (it was for the purpose of putrefaction that the preparations were immersed in horse manure which was renewed when the heat generated by putrefaction diminished). After this time has elapsed, remove the vessel and put it back on the fire until the figures begin to appear in the flask".

This is how Maxwell wished to practise palingenesis of all plants and even of man, and elsewhere he says:[66]

> "And just as in this way the salts of plants are compelled to let appear in a flask the figures of the plants which have prepared these salts, so also, and this is an undoubted fact, the salt of blood (i.e., the salt of the ashes of blood) is in a position to reproduce, under the influence of very little heat, a human figure. And this must be seen as the true homunculus of Paracelsus".

As a counterpart to this palingenesis of shadows, Maxwell also knows the palingenesis of bodies, and thus describes the "true mandrake" of Agrippa!

---

64 *Éclaircissements sur la magie*, II, p. 386.
65 *Medicina magnetica*, I, II, chap. V. – What is in brackets are my comments.
66 *Ob. Cit.*, I, II, ch. XX.

"Mix in a tightly closed and non-artificial vessel (an eggshell emptied by suction), the blood with the noblest particles of the body as well as possible and in the right proportions, and let a hen hatch it. At the end of a certain time you will find, reminiscent of the human form, a mass with which you can do marvellous things; you will also see an oil or liquid which bathes this mass all over. By mixing this oil or liquid with your own sweat, you will, by simple contact, bring about changes in your sense perceptions."

David Van der Becke calls the astral body *Idea seminalis* and gives, in connection with the palingenesis of plants, the following instructions:[67]

"On a calm day, collect the ripe seed of a plant, crush it in a mortar (a pulverising vessel will render the same service),[68] and put it into a flask the size of the plant, with a narrow hole so that it can be tightly closed. Keep the flask closed until an evening when there is hope of heavy dew in the night. Then place the seed in a glass vase and, after putting a tray underneath so that nothing is lost, place it in a meadow or garden so that it is well sprayed, and put it back in the flask before sunrise. Then filter the collected dew and distil it until all deposits are gone. As for the deposit itself, you will calcinate it and after a series of washes you will obtain a salt which you will dissolve in the distilled dew, after which you will pour three fingers high of this distilled dew over the seed impregnated with dew and omit the opening of the flask so that evaporation does not occur. Then keep the flask in a moderately warm place. After a few days, the seed will gradually begin to turn into a kind of mucilaginous earth; the alcohol floating on it will become striated and a green mucilaginous earth membrane will form on its surface.

"Expose the closed flask to the rays of the sun and moon and, in rainy weather, keep it in a warm chamber until all the clues are complete. If you then subject the flask to gentle heat, you will see the image of the plant corresponding to the seed used appear and disappear as it cools. This method of representing the seed idea is used with few variations by all those who practise palingenesis".

Van der Becke also cites palingenesis by means of ashes without, however, giving any instructions in this respect, and believes that in this way a lawful necromancy may be performed with regard to ancestors, provided that some of their ashes have been preserved.[69]

---

67 *Medicina magnetica*, I, II. Chap. XX.
68 Maxwell's observation.
69 *Experimenta*, p. 310.

We find Van der Becke's opinion very complete in its essentials in a work[70] from the end of the last century, which says:

"Take the seed of a plant. The plant can be any plant as long as it is in its maturity and picked by good weather and serene skies. Crush 4 pounds[71] in a glass mortar and pestle and put it into a suitable jar of the size of the whole plant. Then close the jar so that nothing escapes; put it with the crushed seed in a warm place and wait for an evening when the sky is very clear; indeed, as can be seen, it is at such times that the dew gathers in the greatest abundance. Then take the seed to place it in a bowl and expose it to the open air in a garden or meadow. Care should be taken to place the bowl on a wide tray so that nothing is lost in the flow; the dew will fall on the seed and communicate its nature to it. In addition, you should have very clean sheets spread out on the lawn beforehand, on which the dew will be deposited in large quantities, soaking them, so that, by twisting the sheets, the value of eight measures can be collected from this dew and placed in a glass bowl, in only one! As for the seed thus impregnated with dew, it should be placed in the jar before sunrise so that the sun does not reduce it to vapour. It must then be filtered and distilled several times, while the remains of the dew are calcinated to extract the salt. This salt is dissolved in the distilled dew, and is bound to the crushed seed of the bottle until it is twice the width of a finger, and then sealed with wax. The bottle is then buried two feet deep in a damp place or in horse manure for a whole month. If it is then removed, it will be seen that the seed has been transformed and on it will be found a membrane of various colours and, under this membrane, mucilaginous earth, while the dew will appear, owing to the nature of the seed, of a greenish colouring. Hang the closed bottle, throughout the summer, in a place where it can receive the rays of the sun by day and the moon and stars by night. In case of rain or variable weather conditions, it should be kept in a dry place until the weather begins to improve, at which time it can be hung again. Successful work may take two months, or two years, depending on whether the weather has been warm and sunny or not. These are the signs of growth. The mucilaginous matter increases markedly, the alcohol and membrane begin to diminish day by day, and the whole becomes almost massive. There is also seen in the glass, as a result of the reflection of the sun, a subtle vapour, the form or figure, which is that of the plant, floats at this time in an isolated

---

70 *Dissertation sur la résurrection artificielle des animaux, plantes et êtres humains au moyen de leurs cendres*, Francfort and Leipzig, 1785, in-12.

71 It matters little how much. However, it should be noted, as is evident from the following, that two quarts of spray are necessary for every pound of seed.

and colourless nucleus, as well as a simple spider's web.[72] This figure rises and falls frequently depending on the energy with which the sun acts and on whether the moon shines in its full splendour in the sky. Finally, the deposit and the alcohol are transformed into a white ash which, in time, gives rise to the stem, the plant and the flowers, with their colour and shape. If the heat is removed, all this disappears and transforms back into its earth to reappear when the bottle is put back on the fire or when it is kept at a gentle heat. Exposed to the cold again, the figures disappear. If the bottle is tightly closed, the appearance of these figures can continue indefinitely".

Such would be, according to the source quoted, the instructions put into practice by Kircher, on the occasion of which I will point out that Kircher, in maintaining that the Emperor Ferdinand III had received the secret from the Emperor Maximilian, makes a necessarily erroneous statement, since Ferdinand III was born in 1608, while the death of Maximilian II dates from the year 1576.

We also find all of Œttinger's instructions,[73] Becker,[74] very famous in its time, and here are the terms in the German translation:

"Take in due time any plant, or rather every part of it, the root in November, after sowing the seed; the flower in full bloom, the plant before it flowers. Take from all this a notable fraction and dry it in a shady place where neither sun nor any other heat penetrates. Calcinate it all in an earthenware pot with the joints tightly closed and extract the salt with hot water. Next, take the juice from the root of the plant and the flower, put it in an earthenware jar and dissolve the salt in it. After this, take virgin soil, that is, soil that has not yet been ploughed or sown, such as that found in the mountains. This earth should be red, pure and unmixed; pulverise and sieve it. Then put it in a glass or earthen vessel and water it with the above juice until it has absorbed it and begins to turn green. Then place another container on top of it, the height of which corresponds to the natural size of the plant. The joints should be well sealed so that no draughts enter the plant's image. However, the container should be provided with an opening at the lowest part of the container so that air can penetrate the soil. Then expose it to the sun or gentle heat and after half an hour you will see the plant image appear in pearl grey."

---

72 Let us here recall the spider's web appearance which is supposed to be given by the "ghosts", those of the "White Lady", as she is called, and so many other apparitions.
73 Compare with the *Sphinx*, VII, p. 198.
74 *Chymischer Glückshafen*, Frankfurt, 12, in-4, p. 4. This is the German translation of the work, which may be translated as "Happy harbour where chemistry leads."

In the same passage, Becker also communicates the following instructions:

"Grind in a mortar a plant with its roots and flowers, put it in a flask or other vessel until it begins to ferment by itself and gives off heat. Then squeeze out the juice, purify it by filtering it and pour back into the residue what you have filtered to produce the putrefaction as before, until the juice takes on the natural colour of the plant. Then squeeze and filter this juice again, put it in a still and let it digest until all impurities have settled and the juice appears clear, pure and the colour of the plant. Then pour this juice into another still and distil the phlegm and volatile spirits over the top of the still with a gentle heat. The sulphur, i.e. the solid mass of the extract, will remain. Set it aside. From the phlegm, then remove, by distillation over a gentle fire, the ammoniacal volatile products, lighter than water, from the fermentation; set them aside. Next, take the residue, burn it over a low heat and, by means of phlegm, extract the volatile salt (i.e. the ammoniacal salts bound to the acid products of combustion). Again, the phlegm is distilled in a water bath to extract the volatile salt and the residue is calcined until it turns white as ash. Pour the phlegm over the residue and wash off the fixed salt. Filter the lye several times and evaporate the phlegm or purified salt. Then take the two salts, the volatile and the fixed, and pour over them the volatile spirits with the sulphur and the spirits of fire that come first during the distillation, and let it all combine with each other. Instead of the phlegm, you can take distilled rainwater and dissolve in it instead of the fixed salt (potassium carbonate), any vegetable salt, then add the sulphur, coagulate (dry) by means of a slow fire, and thus you will achieve the meeting and combination of the three principles. Put these three principles in a large flask and add the water distilled by the plant itself or the alcohol from the May dew or rainwater. Only one of these two liquids may be sufficient. Subject the hermetically sealed vase to a gentle heat and you will see how the immaterial plant grows with its flowers in this water and appears visibly as long as the heat lasts; it will disappear as it cools and reappear if you heat it, and this is a great miracle of nature and of art".

In the Rosicrucian manuscripts of my great-grandfather[75] are two similar instructions on the palingenesis of bodies and the palingenesis of shadows. The former is attributed to Albertus Magnus and appears in the *A.B.C. d'or des phénomènes de la Nature d'Albert le Grand*, a manuscript pamphlet, the obvious translation of an ancient Latin original. I cannot say whether this pamphlet is in Jammy's great edition of the works of Albert the Great, as this collection is not

---

75 See *Sphinx*, vol. I, p. 45 ff.

at my disposal. However, the original authenticity of the above–mentioned pamphlet seems to me probable for two reasons.

Firstly, the printed works of Albertus Magnus[76] show that this great scholar was familiar with palingenesis, and secondly, it is quite possible, as is often the case, that actually existing manuscripts were not admitted to the collection because the collector was unaware of their existence. The first of these instructions is as follows:

> "Just as in some minerals the *Spiritus Universi* can be found, just as from some minerals a *Spiritum universalem* can be derived; just as among all minerals two are found, which by themselves furnish this *Spiritum*. One is *Minera bismuthi*[77] which comes from the mountains, the other is a brown mineral earth found in silver ores and which contains a similar wonderful life-giving spirit. Pebbles found in rivers also give such a *Liquorem*; but only suitable for making metals grow, because, immersed in this liquor, they grow in height.

> "This is how *Spiritum* is obtained from bismuth. Take *Minera bismuthi* as extracted from the mountains, reduce it by grinding it to an impalpable powder and put this powder in a well-polished retort. Immerse this retort in a vessel full of iron filings, so that it is completely covered by them, and fit it with a coil; then you will draw a *Spiritum per gradus ignis* in forty-eight hours, which will overflow like tears from the eyes. We do not here recommend the use of water; but as the dew[78] furnish the *Spiritum Universi* which in my writings I have called *spiritus roris majalis*, of which you shall add half a pound, for it is not at all contrary to the work. Then add *spiritum bismuthi*. When all is there, put out the fire. When all has cooled, pour the liquor which has overflowed during the distillation into a large still and place it in a *Balneum maris* (water bath) after having covered it with an *Alambicum* (head); then, after having readjusted it, distil; you will obtain a *spiritum* pure as crystal, sweet as honey, this *spiritum* is a living spirit and belongs to *Magic*.

> "This spirit has made me a magician; it is the only active spirit with magical properties that has received from God the Most High the powers it possesses, for it can take all kinds of forms. He is *animal*, because he created *Animalia*; he is vegetable, because he created *Vegetabilia*. Through it grow the trees, the foliage, the grasses, the flowers, yea, all *Vegetabilia*; it is mineral, because it is the principle of all minerals and metals; it is astral, because it comes from above and from below, from the stars with which it

---

76 Eckartshausen, *Éclaircissements sur la magie*, II, p. 388 and 390.
77 It seems to be oxidised bismuth.
78 Compare the following instruction.

is consequently imbued; it is universal, because it is created from the beginning; it is the Word, because it is from God; it is therefore intelligible and the *Primum mobile* of all things; it is pure nature, which comes from light and fire, and then conveys itself and breathes itself into the inner things. Hermes[79] says of these things that the spirit enters them in the bosom of the winds. This spirit takes away and gives life and with it wonders can be performed. This is how:

"Take a plant, a flower or a fruit before nature has made it fully ripe, bunches of grapes, pears, apples, cherries, plums, almonds, for example. After sorting these things, hang them together in the shade and, like flowers, let them dry out. They will then blossom and green up again in midwinter, to the point of ripening and producing their most succulent tasting fruit. Here's how it's done. Take a narrow-mouthed, wide-bellied vessel into which you will pour a pound's worth of the universal spirit; then you will put into this vessel the branches with the flowers and fruits, and seal it with wax so that the spirit will remain in the vessel. Then let the operation proceed by itself. In twenty-four hours everything will begin to turn green and grow: the fruit will ripen, the flowers will take on their fragrance and everything will have a good smell and taste. In this, the power of God will be recognised where the Bishop of Passau[80] sees only a bad work, because he ignores the divine power. This spirit is capable of much more, as the Holy Father himself will see. We must praise and pray to God for all the blessings and miracles He gratifies us, poor human beings that we are. Truly, and who would deny it; it is supernatural to revive dead things in this way by this spirit, which also serves to give proof that this spirit has the power to bring back into existence all that is dead. Thus, having taken a bird and having incinerated it in a vase, I put its ashes in a vessel of this kind (in the manuscript is reproduced, surmounted by a false head, a still in which a liquid can be seen and in it the face of a child). In another vessel, I put the ashes of the decomposing corpse of a small child, after having first reddened the earth in this vessel, and in yet another the ashes of a burnt plant with its flowers. I then filled these different vessels completely with *spiritus*, and let the operation take place by itself. The spirit (astral body) of the child and the plant, developed in twenty-four hours, showed itself to me the *spiritus* with all the appearances of reality. Is this not a true resurrection of these beings? The spirit (here the *spiritus*) awakens the form to such an extent that one can thus have an idea of the appearance we shall assume when we

---

79 In the *Smaragdine Tablet* (Emerald Tablet).
80 Rüdiger of Radeck or Otto of Lomsdorf; both were contemporaries of Albertus.

ourselves are spirits with pure bodies, that is to say, transparent and different in figure.

"Just as the body will receive a new life with the soul and spirit that belong to it, so we too will then be in this transfiguration in a state of contemplation of God, for he is a luminous force. I wanted to say that here I possess a spirit with which I could entertain myself for a few hours a day, but this spirit is only the non-material representation of how we will rise from the dead.

"During a judicial investigation, they found in my house a container in which I had kept the liquor with a drop of the blood of Thomas (Thomas Aquinas, pupil of Albertus), who also has with him a drop of my blood; if you want to know how a dear friend is, you can be informed day and night by this means. If this friend has fallen ill, the little glow in the centre of this vessel, instead of being bright, will emit a very faint glow; if he is very ill, it becomes opaque; if he is angry, the flask becomes hot; if he is agitated, the glow becomes agitated; when he dies, it goes out and the flask bursts. Moreover, one can, since everything comes from this one spirit, use these signs to speak to his friend, for this spirit has all the power."

The Paracelsians and Rosicrucians were much occupied with these vital lamps, and a certain Burggraf published[81] a special book on this subject, which Van Helmont mentions,[82] but which I have not yet been able to find anywhere.

Finally, I would like to report an experience of palingenesis which is recorded in the *Testamentum Fratrum Rosae Aureae Crucis*. It can be compared with the previous one, and for a chemist with a laboratory, it is easy to perform:

"How to prepare *Universal* with dew, rain and white frost.

"My dear children! Let the zeal of work animate you from the beginning of the year. Gather into a large barrel such white frost, snow, mist, dew, and rainwater as you can procure, leave all these things to their own devices, and let them decay and rot until July. You will have real signs when the mass of earth ceases to be homogeneous, when a sort of green membrane forms on top, while the green strength of the vegetation is revealed by the appearance of some worms. My children! When it gets to this point, get to work, stir and mix it all together, then pour it into a coil (alembic with its coil) and simmer distil the 100 pounds, 10 at a time, no more, until the putrefied water is exhausted. Then put the product of the first distillation back

---

81 Burogravis, *De lampade vitæ*, Francf. 1611.
82 V. Helimont, *De magnetica vulnerum curatione*, 20.

into a coil and distil again for 10 pounds.[83] When you have only 10 pounds in all, take a strong retort capable of bearing fire well, and pour these 10 pounds into it; then, in the ashes, over a slow fire, reduce by distillation these 10 pounds to 6, put the *spiritum* back into a retort, immerse it in a water bath, and reduce it by distillation to 3 pounds. At this point, the seventh distillation, it will arouse a very volatile spirit which is pure air; much more, a life-giving spirit, for, if the value of a full teaspoonful is absorbed, the effects of its power will be felt in all the members; it animates the heart and passes through the body like a breath and a spirit. Therefore, you must have rectified this spirit seven times, and thus have pushed it to its ultimate end. Then you can make it serve different purposes and perform miracles with it, for this spirit awakens all things and calls them to life.

"Now take the ashes of a plant, of a flower and of a root, or the ashes of an animal, of a bird or of a lizard, or the ashes of the putrefied corpse of a small child, burn them red hot, and then put them into a large tall flask, or into any other large vessel; and then, with that wonderful life-giving spirit, pour out to the height of a hand and carefully close your vessel, and then put it in a warm place without shaking it. After three times twenty-four hours, the plant will appear with its flower, the animal or child with all its limbs, results which some use for great juggling. These beings, however, are purely spiritual creatures, for, with a little stirring, they soon disappear. If the vessel is left at rest, they reappear, which is a wonderful sight to see, a sight which makes us witness the resurrection of the dead, and shows us how all things in nature will reappear at the time of the universal resurrection.

"My friend! Then it was a dried, wilted flower, or other foliage, a blade of grass or a bunch of grapes that I cut with its stalk and leaves to let them dry in the shade; it is another bunch that I have made from all kinds of unripe fruits as well as from others in the stage of development. Well, when I wanted my pupils to see, I put these twigs, these flowers, in a container and poured over them the necessary quantity of spirit. The container was to be wide at the bottom and narrow at the top. I closed this container at the top with wax and let it stand still for twenty-four hours. At the end of this time, everything began to green up and blossom again, so much so that the dried fruits came to life again even in the dead of winter and even, after three or four days and as many nights, ripened and acquired an exquisite taste. I said then that I had received them from such and such a country to those who were in absolute ignorance of these things.

---

83 As in the rectification of spirits, the total of these distillation products is reduced by successive distillation to ten pounds.

"My friend, I also put some of this spirit in a beautiful little white bottle and added a few drops of my blood or the blood of a dear friend. Then I put a tight lid on the bottle. In this way I could constantly observe how my friend was doing, whether he was healthy, unhappy or happy, because his personality is very characteristic. If he lives happily, there is brightness in the bottle and everything around him is alive,[84] if he is in danger, everything around him is dull; if he is ill, there is darkness and restlessness in the bottle; if he dies naturally or by violent death, the bottle bursts. Thus, with this life-giving spirit, many wonders can be done."

Translated into French by L. Desvignes

---

84 I.e., around the brightness represented by the friend (Translator's note).

PART THREE

Small Dictionary of Botany

This dictionary contains, in addition to the names of each plant, an indication of its qualitative, planetary and zodiacal elemental correspondence, its uses, its special preparation, if any, and its instructions for use.

The time of harvesting is always indicated by the planet and the zodiacal sign, i.e., harvesting should be done when the planet is in the indicated sign.

Of course, we have only mentioned a limited number of plants;[1] this small dictionary is only provided to supply examples for the theories previously exposed.

See *Planetary and Zodiacal symbols* in the **Glossary** in case you need help to identify them.

Acacia (genus of trees of the family *Fabaceae*) – ☿. Sacred tree of the Egyptians and Freemasonry.

Aconite (also called monk's-hood and wolfsbane) (*Aconitum napellus*). – Cold and dry; ♑ ♄. The Greeks said that this plant was born from the dregs of Cer-

---

berus when Hercules brought him out of the underworld. The leaves cure buboes and old ulcers, as well as its root collected in conjunction with ♄ and ☉ infused in wine. It is poisonous, sudorific, good against paralysis, stone, grit, jaundice, asthma; it stops nosebleeds, makes hair grow back; it is an antidote for poisonous bites. – One of the twelve Rosicrucian plants.

AGAR TREE (also called wood of gods, agar tree, aguru, sachi-pat, sanchi, hasi, agil and akil) (*Aquilaria malaccensis*). – ♂ in ♏. Febrifuge (Annam).

AGARIC (this name is given to several mushrooms, including both edible and poisonous species. To this genus belong widely cultivated species, such as the common mushroom: *Agaricus bisporus*). – Hot, dry, slightly moist, ♑. Harvest at the end of July and beginning of August.

AGATE (also called vegetable hummingbird, agati in Tamil and Agase in Kannada and Avisa in Telugu or hummingbird tree) (*Sesbania grandiflora*). – ☉ in ♋. The chewed bark is good against asthma.

AGRIMONY (also called common agrimony, church steeples and sticklewort) (*Agrimonia eupatoria*). – Cold and dry, ♉ or ♒. Grows in hedges and bushes. Astringent leaves, effective against angina, nephritis, weak bladder. Placed under the head of a sleeping person, prevents waking. When fumigated it drives away evil spirits; in lotions it is good against ocular cataracts (Dioscorides), dislocations and sprains; vermifuge; good against snakebites, sheep cough, etc. (O. de Serres).

ALDER TREE (also called common alder, black alder, European alder and European black alder) (*Alnus glutinosa*). – ☽. Used for making magic wands; charcoal made from its wood is used in evocations.

ALEXANDERS (also called alisander, horse-parsley and wild-parsley) (*Smyrnium olusatrum*). – Has the same properties as celery.

ALMOND TREE (*Prunus dulcis*). – ☿ and ♃. Five or six bitter almonds taken on an empty stomach prevent the effects of drunkenness. These fruits are good for consumptives, wet-nurses and the impotent; they are soothing for all inflammations; they are taken with eggs for bronchitis.

ALOE (the tribe of *Aloeae* is in the family *Asphodelaceae*, subfamily *Asphodeloideae*, its most widely known species is *Aloe vera*, or "true aloe"). – ☉ ♐. Aloe powder is used as a perfume to attract ♃ influences. A decoction of aloe wood is good for facilitating conception. Lotions of aloe juice and vinegar prevent hair loss, in tincture, it forms the long life elixir of Codex.

Amaranth (A plant of the genus *Amaranthus*). – ♃. Its flower is the symbol of immortality; wreaths made with this flower conciliate to those who wear them the favour of the great and glory.

Angelica (also called garden angelica, wild celery, and Norwegian angelica) (*Angelica archangelica*). – Hot and dry, ♌ or ♒, ☉; collected when ☽ is in ☿ and ♓, or at the end of August. Good against fascinations; hung around the necks of small children it preserves them from evil spells. For the latter uses, the wild species, marked by ♐ is less active; it has the same virtues as verbena against rabies; stimulant, stomachic, emmenagogue. The leaves, under the dominion of ♄, collected when it is at its house, are good against gout. The root, under the dominion of ☉ and ♂, collected when these stars are in ♌, cures gangrene and poisoned bites. The juice of the leaves, put on decayed teeth, relieves pain. A decoction of the root taken on an empty stomach in the morning cures inveterate coughs. Infusion in wine cures internal ulcerations and rabies.

Anise (also called aniseed) (*Pimpinella anisum*). – Warm and moist; ♊, or ♏, ☿. The berries are antiparasitic. Its oil and water are good for acute colic in small children. They should be used by wet nurses. Carminative, digestive, purgative; in lotions, improves eyesight; infused in wine with saffron, cures ophthalmia; fragments of this plant, macerated in water and introduced into the nostrils, cure nasal ulcers.

Annual mercury (also known as garden mercury and French mercury) (*Mercurialis annua*). – Cold and wet; ♍. The juice, taken in decoction by a woman for four days, facilitates the conception of a male child, if a male plant has been used, or of a female child, if a female plant has been used. Purging.

Apple tree (*Malus domestica*). – Cold and moderately dry, ♏. Dedicated to Ceres; the wood is ♏, ♃: the fruit is signed by ♀; when a lover dreams that he eats it, it means that he will soon be happy. The apple bears the sign of Adam's fall.

Artichoke (also called globe artichoke; known as French artichoke and green artichoke in North America) (*Cynara scolymus*). – ♂ in ♏. Aphrodisiac. The root or seed collected when ☉ is in the 5th degree of , cures the fluxes of the belly or blood. The water of its fluff is good for the hair.

ARUM (the genus *Arum*, of the family *Araceae* includes numerous species, with the greatest diversity in the Mediterranean area). – ♓ o ♍. Moist and a little hot; ♂ Emollient.

ASH TREE (its different varieties belong to the genus *Fraxinus*, part of the family *Oleaceae*). – Cold and dry, ♉ or ♍; flowers are ♒; ♃ or ☉. The leaves, chewed, are good against the bites of poisonous animals and rheumatism; the bark is very febrifuge. – According to Paracelsus, if one makes a virgin child pick a branch, when ♄ is in ♏, this branch will cure pains, gout and dry sores. The root revives turquoise.

ASPARAGUS (also called sparagus, sperage, garden asparagus and sparrow grass) (*Asparagus officinalis*). – Warm and moist. ♈, pick when the ☉ and ☽ are in ♋. Diuretic and aphrodisiac. The shoots soothe heart palpitations.

BANANA TREE (also called plantain) (belongs to several types of large herbaceous plants of the genus *Musa*). – ☾ in ♓. The flowers are used against blennorrhagia (east).

BANYAN TREE (also called banyan fig and Indian banyan) (*Ficus benghalensis*). – ♃ in ♍. Sacred tree of the Hindus.

BARBERRY (also known as common barberry and European barberry) (*Berberis vulgaris*). – ♃ and ♂. Cures diarrhoea, dysentery, angina, jaundice, blood flow; berries make the consequences of drunkenness disappear.

BARLEY (*Hordeum vulgare*). – ☉. Ears, Yava (Sanskrit) are offered by Brahmins as a sacrifice to the gods and the seven spiritual princes. – Refreshes the blood, diuretic.

BASIL (also called great basil) (*Ocimum basilicum*). – Warm and dry; ♌; ♂; collected when ☉ is in ♓ and ☽ in ♋. Emblem of anger. – On this plant, ♂ opposes ♄ and their fight is activated by ☿; ♀ and ♃, who come last. – The sorcerers used it because it gives a pestilential lunar menstruation; but it can be worked in such a way that ☿ drives the poison under the regime of ♀; then ♂ is transformed into

☉, and the raging fire of the plant becomes a fire of love. The smell drives away mosquitoes.

BAY TREE (also known as bay, bay laurel, sweet bay, true laurel and Grecian laurel) (*Laurus nobilis*). – Hot and dry, ♌ ☉. Picked when the ☉ is at ♓ and ☾ at ♒. The berries are from ♏, vermifuge. The chewed leaves are good against poisonous animal bites. – All parts of the tree are antimicrobial. The ancient soothsayers crowned themselves with its leaves and chewed them: that is why they were called Daphnephages.[2] It is the instrument of the art called *Daphnomancy*, by which omens are extracted from the crackling, sparks and smoke produced by its burning branches. The whole bush has the virtue of warding off lightning. To learn more about the subject, study the myth of *Daphne*. The juice of the leaves, taken in a dose of 3 or 4 drops in water, brings on menstruation, corrects stomach crudity, improves deafness and earaches, erases spots on the face. Worn on the body, the leaves prevent infernal visions. The berries, picked at the time of ♂ and ♀, powdered, put in wine, are good against colic.

BEANS (Sédir does not specify which type of bean he is referring to, he uses the generic word fèves meaning broad beans; legume family in the order *Fabales*). – ♋, ♄ and ☿. Harvested at the end of October they are under ♏ with ☿. The fruit is signed by ♄ and ☽. The decoction of the roasted grains is good against grit and stone; the poultice of its flour resolves tumours of the sexual parts and passes tanning of the face. The flowers bear the sign of hell according to the school of Pythagoras.

BEAR'S BREECHES (also called sea dock, bear's foot plant, sea holly and oyster plant) (*Acanthus mollis*). – ♂. Emollient.

BEECH, COMMON (also known as beech tree and European beech) (*Fagus sylvatica*). – ♃ ♄. The bark of young trees is febrifuge, vermifuge and aperient.

BELLADONNA (also called deadly nightshade) (*Atropa belladonna*). – Cold and wet; ♍; narcotic; useful in spasmodic, nervous and epileptic contractions.

BETONY (also called common hedgenettle, purple betony, wood betony, bishopwort, and bishop's wort) (*Betonica officinalis*). – Hot and dry, ♓ in ♃. Harvested when the full moon marks the end of the canicular days. Sternutatory; its leaves purify the blood; good against jaundice and dropsy, as well as against spells.

---

2   Soothsayers who, before answering questions put to them, ate laurel leaves, because, as this tree was consecrated to Apollo, they believed themselves to be inspired by this god.

Bindweed (the term used by Sédir is liseron, which is an ambiguous vernacular name in French for certain herbaceous perennial plants with a more or less fleshy rhizome, of the family *Convolvulaceae*, with voluble stems and arrow-shaped leaves). – ☿. Dedicated to Saint Peter.

Birch (*Betula pubescens*). – ♃ in ♐. In Kamchatka it is used in one of their sacred ceremonies, the broom festival; witches in the Middle Ages also used it to go to the Sabbath or coven, to make rain come, etc. The smell of this tree is good for melancholic people and victims of witchcraft. The juice of its leaves prevents worms from entering the cheese.

Bistort (also known as snakeweed, snakeroot, snake-root, Easter-ledges, english serpentary, dragon-wort, osterick and passions) (*Bistorta officinalis*). – Cold and dried, ♏, or ♒, ♄, ☿; chewing it or putting the juice on the wound cures snakebite. The smell of the root is very effective in charming snakes. Good in gargle for accidents of the respiratory organs. It is one of the most adept at becoming an accumulator of astral fluids, in any form. – Very astringent, against all fluxes, aphthous ulcers, etc.

Bittersweet nightshade (also known as amara dulcis, bittersweet and woody nightshade) (*Solanum dulcamara*). – Purifies by perspiration, all decompositions of humours,[3] even cancerous, and strong bruises (poultices).

Black bamboo (*Phyllostachys nigra*). – Used instead of verbena by black people (Stanislas de Guaita, Temple of Satan, Ouroboros, 2020.).

Black elder (also known as elder, elderberry, European elder, European elderberry and European black elderberry) (*Sambucus nigra*). – Hot and dry, ♈, ☿. Can be collected under ♌. It is the emblem of zeal. ☿. The oil extracted from its seeds, or in which they are infused, is good against gout; the mistletoe of the elder, which grows with the willows, is specific against epilepsy; the flowers cure erysipelas and burns; the seed is sudorific; its bark is good for dropsy. A small stem picked just before the new moon in October and cut into nine pieces is excellent for dropsy, as is its root, picked by pulling it down on St. John the Baptist's Day at noon. The water from the leaves kills flies (Alexis Piémontois).

Black hawthorn (also called European buckthorn and Mediterranean buckthorn) (*Rhamnus lycioides*). – Hot and dry, ♎; consecrated to Saturn. – It was used to weave Christ's crown of thorns, symbolises virginity, sin, the devil, hu-

---

3   By *humours* it means the four bodily fluids called humours: blood, phlegm, melancholy and anger.

mility; its branches hanging from the doors and windows of a house stop the efforts of sorcerers and demons. – Purging.

BLACK NIGHTSHADE (also known as European black nightshade and common nightshade) (*Solanum nigrum*). – For all festering wounds and boils.

BLACK SPLEENWORT (*Asplenium adiantum-nigrum*). – ♄. It was the crown of Pluto. For bronchial tubes.

BLACKBERRY (also known as bramble and black-berry bush) (*Rubus fruticosus*). – ♋, consecrated to Saturn; emblem of envy; its leaves are good for the mouth.

BLACKCURRANT (also known as black currant and cassis) (*Ribes nigrum*). – The juice of the leaves is useful against poisonous bites.

BLACKTHORN (also known as sloe and sloe-bush) (*Prunus spinosa*). – The fruit is subject to ♓; the tree to ♏, makes the consequences of drunkenness disappear.

BLADDER-SENNA (*Colutea arborescens*). – The leaves are labelled ♎.

BLESSED THISTLE (also known as St. Benedict's thistle, holy thistle, spotted thistle and Cardo bendito) (*Cnicus benedictus*). – ♂ in ♌. Harvested in June, before the yellow flowers bloom. More potent febrifuge than quinine; taken macerated in a small glass of white wine. Diuretic, sudorific, depurative, detersive. The dew collected in its capsules is good for scrofulous and catarrhal ophthalmia. Its infusion cures lung ulcers.

BOG-ROSEMARY (*Andromeda polifolia*). – (Alps) ♄ pungent, narcotic for cattle.

BORAGE (also called starflower and is also known bee plant or bee bread because its blue purplish star shaped flower attracts bees all summer long) (*Borago officinalis*). – Warm and moist, ♓ or ♃ in ♒; purifies the blood, diuretic.

BOXWOOD (also called common box and European box) (*Buxus sempervirens*). – Warm and dry, ♌ or ♎. Pick it when ☉ is at ♓ and ☽ at ♒. Consecrated to Ceres, or to Cybele because they made flutes out of them.

BRANCHED ASPHODEL (*Asphodelus ramosus*). – ♄. Used in evocations.

BROOM (also known as common broom and Scotch broom) (*Cytisus scoparius*). – Warm and dry, ♌. Harvested in ☉ and ☽ in ♒; berries are subject to ♍ and consequently antiparasitic; flowers are diuretic and cardiac.

BRYONIA (also known as bryonia, white bryonia, and countless other names) (*Bryonia alba*). – ☿ in ♌. Climbing plant; has the virtue of protecting from lightning (Columelle).

BUCKWHEAT (also called common buckwheat) (*Fagopyrum esculentum*). – Cold and dry, ♃, ♏, especially its leaves and roots. All species are detersive and vulnerary. Paracelsus uses it with turpentine essence and earthworms; in distilled water, or as a poultice with comfrey (*Symphytum officinale*) and aloe. Also is pulmonary, diuretic and menstrual. In lotion in wine it dries out scabies and washes wounds. The smoke of its seeds relieves epileptics, the possessed and the impotent (Apuleius).

BUCK'S-HORN PLANTAIN (also known as stagshorn plantain, minutina and erba stella) (*Plantago coronopus*). – ♂. Spraying and infusion cause bleeding.

BUGLOSS (also called alkanet and orchanet) (*Anchusa officinalis*). – Dry and cold, ♉ ♃. Purifies the blood; root is diuretic; good for heart palpitations and dropsy.

BUTTERCUP (the buttercups –*Ranunculus* genus– are herbaceous annual or perennial plants of the family *Ranunculaceae*). – Warm and dry, ♌; collected when the ☉ is on ♌ with the ☾ on ♍ or the ☉ on ♉ with the ☾ on ♓.

CABBAGE (also known as colewort: wild cabbage) (*Brassica oleracea*). – The cabbage is harvested at the end of October as ♋. Good for stomach inflammations; seeds are antiparasitic.

CALAMINT (also known as lesser calamint, mountain-mint, mill mountain, mountain balm and basil thyme) (*Clinopodium nepeta*). – The crushed leaves, infused in white wine, are a tonic against hallucinations (Dioscorides).

CAMELLIA (also called common camellia Japanese camellia and tsubaki) (*Camellia japonica*). – ♍. The distilled plant yields an oil that can be preserved to supply worship lamps.

CAMPHOR TREE (also called camphorwood and camphor laurel) (*Cinnamomum camphora*). – ☽. Burnt resin (camphor) gives a lunar aroma.

CANNABIS. See **HEMP**.

CAPER SPURGE (also called paper spurge, gopher spurge, gopher plant and mole plant) (*Euphorbia lathyris*). – Hot and dry, ♈. It is collected in ♌.

CARADONNA (also called woodland sage, Balkan clary, blue sage and wild sage) (*Salvia nemorosa*). – Cold and dried, ♍ or ♒.

CARAWAY (also called meridian fennel and Persian cumin) (*Carum carvi*). – ☉ in ♓. The seed is used as a stomachic; it is put in food. The smoke is very good as a magic perfume.

CARDAMOM (also called green cardamom and true cardamom) (*Elettaria cardamomum*). – The medium-sized or small ones are from ☉ en ☽. Seeds are aromatic, stomachic, etc.

CARROT (*Daucus carota subsp. sativus*). – For jaundice, diphtheria, canker sores, skin diseases.

CASTOR OIL PLANT (also known as castor bean and castor plant) (*Ricinus communis*). – Warm, moist, ♃ or ♓. Can be collected under ♌. Prevents fascination, bewitchment and sudden fright.

CATNIP (also known as catswort, catwort and catmint) (*Nepeta cataria*). – ☿. Collected under a favourable aspect, it can, if the active principle can be extracted from it, bestow a revival of vitality.

CEDAR (the genus *Cedrus* has three or four species of cedars, depending on the classification). – ♃. Emblem of pride.

CELERY (also called smallage and ajamoda) (*Apium graveolens*). – ☿ in ♌. Sacred and funerary plant of the Greeks; the seeds are digestive and carminative. Diuretic. Detersive; cleanses wounds, deflates the breasts of wet nurses.

CENTUREA (popular name for several plants, mainly knapweed, *Centaurea nigra* and centaury, *Centaurium erythraea*). – Hot and dry, ♌, ♃. Collected when ☉ is at ♉ and ☽ at ♓ or at the end of August, or when ♃ is at ♐ with ♄ and ♂. Legend has it that it was discovered by the centaur Chiron. It is useful against jaundice, colic, biliary fevers, gout, scurvy, worms, and is good for menstruation. Anti-demoniac (Pliny). From a magical point of view, it is a plant whose virtue is exalted when, before picking it, words of incantation are pronounced over it. If it is mixed with oil from a lamp and a little blood from a female hoopoe, it will give hallucinations to those present. If one throws it into the fire and then looks at the sky, the stars will appear to move; if one makes someone breathe it, they will be afraid.

Chamomile (also called camomile, German chamomile, Hungarian chamomile, wild chamomile, blue chamomile and scented mayweed) (*Matricaria chamomilla*). – Moderately hot and moist, ♓ or ♎; ☿. Collected under ♂, conjunction of ☽ and ☉; good against obstructions of humours in thoracic organs, for hysteria and intermittent fevers.

Chard (also called silver beet, perpetual spinach, beet spinach, seakale beet and leaf beet) (*Beta vulgaris var. cicla*). – Cold and moderately dry. ♏. Picked when ☉ is ♋, passes into ♍. Against enteritis.

Chervil (also called French parsley and garden chervil.) (*Anthriscus cerefolium*). – Inwardly, for liver colic, ailments of the breasts and womb and against dropsy; outwardly against all swelling.

Chicory (also known as succory) (*Cichorium intybus*). – Hot and dry; ♈, or ♏. It is collected after the full moon that ends the canicular days. Kneeling, the root is touched with gold and silver, on the day of the nativity of St. John the Baptist, before the sun rises, and then plucked from the earth with oaths, ceremonies and exorcisms with the sword of Judas Maccabaeus.[4] Picked when ♃ is at ♐, the ☉ at ♌ and at ♀ time, it acquires vulnerary and healing properties. Purifies, calms, clears.

Chinaberry tree (also called pride of India, bead-tree, Cape lilac, syringa berrytree, Persian lilac, Indian lilac and white cedar) (*Melia azedarach*). – Cold and dry; ♉.

Chinese lantern (also called Japanese-lantern, strawberry groundcherry and winter-cherries) (*Physalis alkekengi*). – Cold and dry, ♉ or ♎. Diuretic; against dropsy.

Chrysanthemum (also known as garden mum, Queen of autumn and florist's daisy) (*Chrysanthemum morifolium*). – ☿. Good against sorcerers.

Cinnamon tree (also called true cinnamon tree and Ceylon cinnamon tree) (*Cinnamomum verum*). – Cinnamon is the bark from the centre of the branches of the tree; serves as a solar perfume; by distillation a reddish oil or quintessence is obtained, which has a very penetrating taste and is an excellent tonic.

---

4   Thiron d'ap. Pistorius, *Epitome de Magia*, c. 26, 27.

Cinquefoil (also known as five-leaved grass, creeping cinquefoil, European cinquefoil and creeping tormentil) (*Potentilla reptans*). – The root heals wounds and skin conditions, using it as a plaster; suppresses scrofulosis, when its juice is drunk dissolved in water; relieves toothache. When worn on the person, it brings luck, enables one to be heard by the great and opens understanding (Albert the Great).

Clove tree (also called tropical myrtle and Zanzibar redhead) (*Syzygium aromaticum*). – Warm and dry ♌, ☉. Harvested when ☉ is at ♓ and ☽ at ♋. Clove essence is used as a prop in some practical magic work; combined with phosphorus, it feeds larvae; a clove kept in the mouth is a powerful adjuvant for the hypnotist; eating cloves facilitates conception. The oil is good for toothache.

Coca (*Erythroxylum coca* is one of two species of cultivated coca). – ♄ and ☉. – Plant from Peru whose leaves are powerfully tonic and excitant. According to the learned Stanislas de Guaita, hypodermic injections of its salt, cocaine, can become a real pact with astral beings (See *Coca of Peru* in the *Esoteric Glossary*).

Coconut tree (*Cocos nucifera*). – ♃ in ♏. Diuretic root.

Colocynth (also known as bitter apple, bitter cucumber, desert gourd, egusi, vine of Sodom, or wild gourd) (*Citrullus colocynthis*). – Hot and dry; ♈. Can be picked under ♌; it is a species of cucumber.

Coltsfoot (also known as coughwort, foal's-foot, horse-hoof and bull's-foot) (*Tussilago farfara*). – ♄, ♋; against catarrh, asthma; as a drink or tobacco. – Picked after the full moon which ends the canicular days. One of the twelve Rosicrucian plants.

Colza (the name used by Sédir is rave, which is an ambiguous vernacular name in French for certain vegetable or fodder plants grown for their edible roots, in the *Brassica* genus, e.g. *Brassica rapa* –a plant species made up of many subspecies– and *Brassica napus*, rapeseed). – ♏ or ♂ in ♓. Its seed is aphrodisiac; diuretic, anti–poison and good against smallpox.

Comfrey (also known as common comfrey, true comfrey, Quaker comfrey, cultivated comfrey, boneset, knitbone, consound and slippery-root) (*Symphytum officinale*). – ♃ in ♓. Stops bleeding in wounds and vomiting; good for lung ulcers, fractures, rheumatism.

Coriander (also called Chinese parsley and cilantro) (*Coriandrum sativum*). – ♀. Aromatic; used to give a good flavour to beer. Cordial, carminative.

Cornelian cherry (also called European cornel and Cornelian cherry dogwood) (*Cornus mas*). – ♏ or ♃ or ♂. Dedicated to Ares.

Cornflower (also known as bachelor's button and garden cornflower) (*Centaurea cyanus*). – Cold and wet ♓.

Couch grass (also known as dog's-grass, quick grass, quitch grass, quackgrass, scutch grass and witchgrass) (*Elymus repens*). – Against jaundice, nephritis, renal lithiasis and dyspepsia.

Cowslip (also known as common cowslip and cowslip primrose) (*Primula veris*). – Dedicated to St. Peter's. ☿ in ♎, chases away melancholy; its salt is a mild purgative; cures at the same time inflammations of the mouth and tongue.

Creeping Thyme (also known as Breckland thyme, Breckland wild thyme, wild thyme and elfin thyme) (*Thymus serpyllum*). – ☿. Against snakebites.

Cress (also called garden cress and curly cress) (*Lepidium sativum*). – Warm and dry; ♈ or ♐; harvested in early April or under ♏, aphrodisiac.

Cuckoo Pint (also known as snakeshead, adder's root, arum, wild arum and lords-and-ladies) (*Arum maculatum*). – Wood and berries, pungent, asthma-fighting.

Cucumber (*Cucumis sativus*). – ☽; ♐ or ♋. Burnt seeds are used to call upon the powers of the ☽; a snake-shaped cucumber, candied, soaked in water, makes all bedbugs disappear.

Cyclamen (*Cyclamen* it is a genus of tuberous plants). – The root is signed by ♎; the leaf is signed by ♌; the plant is dedicated to Apollo. The water of this plant, with foüs serpentinae or sophiae Sana, gives a good ointment for fistulas. Good for philtres.[5]

Cypress spurge (also called Bonaparte's crown, graveyard spurge, graveyard weed and yellowweed) (*Euphorbia cyparissias*). – ♂ in ♌. Violent purgative. Root infused for three days in vinegar cures dropsy.

Cypress (a tree belonging to the genus *Cupressus*). – Warm and dry. ♌. ♄. It is collected when ☉ is at ♓ and ☽ at ♋; image of death; it crowned the head of Pluto. – Its decoction blackens and preserves hair.

---

5   Generally love potions.

DAFFODIL (daffodils are bulbous plants of the genus *Narcissus*, family *Amaryllidaceae*). – Cold and dry; ♉ or ♌; ♀; from Greek *narké*: numbing; offered to the Furies, and to Pluto. – The distilled water of its root increases the secretion of sperm; in lotion makes firm the breasts; worn on oneself, it attracts the friendship of virgins.

DAISY (also known as common daisy, lawn daisy and English daisy) (*Bellis perennis*). – ☉, ☿. – Good against bruises, scrofula and knots.[6]

DANDELION (also called common dandelion, blowball, dandelion and faceclock) (*Taraxacum officinale* and other *Taraxacum* species). – Tonic; used externally to treat skin conditions.

DANEWORT (also known as dane weed, danesblood, dwarf elder or European dwarf elder, walewort, dwarf elderberry, elderwort and blood hilder) (*Sambucus ebulus*). – Hot and dry. ♒. Harvested after the full moon that ends the canicular days. Leaves are anti-inflammatory; bark is purgative.

DEVIL'S BIT (also known as devil's-bit scabious) (*Succisa pratensis*). – Cold and dry; ♉ or ♎; ☿. The flowers have the signature of ♈. For asthma and chancres.

DITTANY OF CRETE (also called Cretan dittany and hop marjoram) (*Origanum dictamnus*). – ☉ in ♋. Its name comes from a mountain in Crete where it grew in abundance; it is a balsamic, sedative, evergreen plant; the leaves in a compress are good for pregnant women; garlands made from it, or its smoke, develop somnambulistic clairvoyance; it was consecrated to Lucina.

EDELWEISS (also known as snow flower) (*Leontopodium alpinum*). – One of the twelve Rosicrucian plants.

---

6   An indolent, encysted tumour that occurs under the skin and contains rotting or gangrenous material.

ELECAMPANE (also called horse-heal and elfdock) (*Inula helenium*). – Useful against asthma, tuberculosis, leucorrhoea, dyspepsia; externally: scabies; especially the root.

ELM (also known as field elm) (*Ulmus minor*). – ♃, ♂. – The second bark is used in decoction against sciatica.

EYEBRIGHT (also called meadow eyebright, red eyebright and eyewort) (*Euphrasia officinalis*). – Warm and dry. Flowers are signed by ♈.

FARFARA (it is not quite clear which plant this refers to, see **COLTSFOOT**, another plant that may be related to this one). – Warm, dry and moist, ♎ or ♓; collected under ♌.

FAVA BEAN (also known as broad bean and faba bean) (*Vicia faba*). – ♃ in ♒. A herbal tea made from its leaves is good against renal colic.

FENNEL (the word used by Sédir, *fenouil*, meaning fennel, is an ambiguous vernacular name designating, in French, a multitude of plants of various genera, in particular of the family *Apiaceae*, such as common fennel, bastard fennel, etc.). – Warm and humid, ♓ or ♒. The candied umbels purify the breath; the distilled green plant gives a good water for eye inflammations; in infusion, the plant makes menstruation come.

FIELD SAGEWORT (also called field wormwood, beach wormwood, northern wormwood, Breckland wormwood boreal wormwood, Canadian wormwood and field mugwort) (*Artemisia campestris*). – Warm and dry, ♈, it is harvested after the full ☽ which ends the canicular days. Consecrated to St. John the Baptist, good against charms, lightning, evil spirits, epilepsy and the dance of St. Vitus.

FIG TREE (*Ficus carica*). – Moderately warm and moist; ♒. Black is from ♄; white from ♃ and ♀. Dedicated to Mercury or Bacchus by Sparta; in India, it is dedicated to Vishnu; Saturn was crowned with its leaves. A fig branch picked under a suitable aspect calms angry bulls. The fruit is emollient; it is good against corns on the feet: just cover the corns for several days. Sycomancy was a type of divination using fig leaves. The question was written on a leaf, and if the leaf did not dry immediately, it was a bad omen.

FIGWORT (also known as woodland figwort, common figwort and throat-wort) (*Scrophularia nodosa*). – Cold and dry; ♉, ♋ or ♎. If harvested at the end of October, it is signed by ♏. Its leaves are used to treat white tumours.[7]

FLAX (belongs to *Linum*, a genus of angiosperms in the family *Linaceae*, among other species, includes *Linum usitatissimum*, used to produce linseed fibre and linseed oil). – ♃. Soothing; good for pleurisy; ripens ulcers, softens hard tumours.

FORGET-ME-NOTS (the name of the flowers of plants of the genus *Myosotis*; the main species are: *Myosotis arvensis*, *Myosotis alpestri*, *Myosotis scorpioides* and *Myosotis sylvatica*). – Don't forget me. – Cold and dry, ♉.

FOXGLOVE (also known as common foxglove, purple foxglove and lady's glove) (*Digitalis purpurea*). – ♂ in ♓. – Subjected to prolonged distillation, it gives a good liquor for external use in astringent lotions against wounds; and for internal use, in homeopathic doses, against heart palpitations, oppression and uncontrollable vomiting.

FRAGRANT SOLOMON'S SEAL (also known as angular Solomon's seal and scented Solomon's seal) (*Polygonatum odoratum*). – Cold and dry, ♉ or ♍ or also ♑. For whitlows and viper bites.

FRANKINCENSE (produced from the resin of a group of trees of the genus *Boswellia*, especially *Boswellia sacra* and *Boswellia thurifera*). – Generated by the sun from the body of Leucothoe, his lover. – It is a resin that gives a solar perfume, acting on the soul centre.

FUCHSIA (*Fuchsia* is a genus of flowering plants, of the family *Onagraceae*, within the order *Myrtales*). – ♀ in ♌. One of the twelve plants of the Rosicrucians.

FUMITORY (also known as common fumitory, drug fumitory and earth smoke) (*Fumaria officinalis*). – ♃, ♄ and ♂. Purgative, desiccant; good against scabies and syphilis.

---

7   Such as abscesses, boils, boils, pannadices, acne, etc.

Garlic (*Allium sativum*). – ♂ ♐. The Egyptians honoured this plant; the Greeks forbade entry into the Temple of the Mother of the Gods to anyone who had eaten it; should be used by correcting it by ♄ (vinegar); on an empty stomach, preserves from evil spells; diuretic, vermifuge, expectorant and menstrual. Good against dropsy, stone. Hang a box of garlic from a tree, or wipe it with an instrument rubbed with garlic to keep birds away. – For odourless garlic, plant it and pick it when the moon is no longer below the horizon.

Gentian (a name applied to several members of the same family. The French name, *gentiane*, designates many species of the family *Gentianaceae*). – Warm and dry; ♈ or ♌, ☉. It can be collected under ♌ or ♉ with ☽ in ♓. The species growing in the mountains was used by the Rosicrucians. Dedicated to St. Peter. The root is febrifuge and anti-scorbutic.

Germander (also known as tree germander, bush germander and shrubby germander) (*Teucrium fruticans*). – Warm and dry; ♈ is collected under ♌.

Goat's beard (also called buck's-beard and bride's feathers) (*Aruncus dioicus*). – Hot and humid ♎.

Greater burdock (also known as edible burdock, lappa, beggar's buttons, thorny burr and happy major) (*Arctium lappa*). – ♄ in ♍. Its root, collected at new moon, when the sun is at ♍, cures toothache; collected at full moon, it is a good remedy against inflammations, its powdered leaves are useful against old ulcers.

Greater celandine (also known as celandine, nipplewort, swallowwort and tetterwort) (*Chelidonium majus*). – Cold and dry, ♉ or ♎. Good against corns.

Greater dodder (also known as European dodder) (*Cuscuta europaea*). – ♄ and ♃. Cures obstructions and venereal diseases.

Ground ivy (also known as alehoof, cat's-foot, ground-ivy, gill-go-by-ground, gill-creep-by-ground, turn-hoof and haymaids) (*Glechoma hederacea*). Good for all chest complaints; soothes labour pains in poultices.

HARMAL (also known as Syrian rue, harmala, harmel, wild rue, African rue and esfand) (*Peganum harmala*). – Warm and slightly dry; ♓ or ♎, also ♐; ♄, ♂ and ☉. Crushed with sage in vinegar, it cures quartan fevers; vermifuge, against iron deficiency anaemia.[8] Its seeds are called Harmel; it is believed to have been the moly[9] that Mercury made Ulysses take to prevent him from Circe's concoctions. If it is taken when ♄ is weak and ☉ is in the X house, it preserves from spells. – A sprig of harmal tied under the wing of a hen preserves her from the cat and fox. When a room is sprinkled with its decoction mixed with mare's urine, fleas disappear immediately (Pliny). Emmenagogue.

HART'S-TONGUE (also known as hart's-tongue fern) (*Asplenium scolopendrium*). – Hot and dry. ♈.

HASHISH. See **HEMP**.

HAZELNUT TREE (also known as common hazel, European filbert, European hazelnut and cobnut) (*Corylus avellana*). – ♋ or ♎; ♃ or ☿. The spirit of hazel wood, prepared under a conjunction of ☽ and ☿ is excellent for the sight. Twigs collected in a suitable aspect can be used for ceremonial magic and rhabdomancy. – ☿. Hazelnuts can heal dislocations of the limbs by sympathy, if the will of the operator is strong enough, by gathering two almonds and carrying them around.

HEATH SPOTTED-ORCHID (also known as moorland spotted orchid and satyrion) (*Dactylorhiza maculata*). – Cold and wet, ♏ or ♀ in ♌. Aphrodisiac; Kircher tells in his *Ars magna*, vol. II, 2, ch. v, the story of a young man who suffered from satyriasis while walking in a garden full of this plant.

HEATHER (belongs to the genus *Erica*, of the family *Ericaceae*; the most common species in Europe is *Erica cinerea*, or bell heather). – ☿ in ♐. Good for divination.

HELIOTROPE (also known as potato weed, caterpillar weed, turnsole, European turn-sole, heliotropium and European heliotrope) (*Heliotropium europaeum*). – In ♌. Consecrated to Apollo; one of the twelve magical plants of the Rosicrucians; if a sleepwalker is magnetised with a stalk of this plant picked at the right

---

8　Anaemia due to lack of iron in young girls.
9　Plant of which Homer speaks and to which he attributes marvellous virtues.

time, the sleepwalker will give true revelations; it can give indications in dreams about thieves. If it is placed in a church where there are women, those who have been unfaithful to their husbands will not be able to leave (Albert the Great).

Hellebore (hellebores are rhizomatous perennial plants of the family *Renonculaceae*). – The black hellebore (*Helleborus niger*), the seed of which is called Mondella, is signed by ♑ or ♄. The pulverised root is used as a perfume in the corresponding magical operations. Macerated in spirit of wine, then distilled over a slow fire, gives a liquor to which nib sugar is added; taken in pure water where hypoglossus has been steeped,[10] is a specific against epilepsy (Paracelsus). The oil of the root is also good. – White hellebore (*Veratrum album*), with red flowers, is warm and dry; ♋; collected in early April or under ♍; a sternutatory; given to horses and black sheep; violent purgative. Best species is the one with red flowers tending to white; should be collected in favourable ♃ and ☽ light. Good topical for the elderly, the hydropic and the lunatic, used as a dry powder; melancholic people are relieved by carrying the root with them.

Hemlock (also known as poison hemlock, deadly hemlock and poison parsley) (*Conium maculatum*). – Cold, dry and also wet; ♍; or ♒; ♄; should be collected when ♄ is in conjunction with ☉, then it is anti-aphrodisiac, its water cures rheumatism and prevents breast overgrowth. Poisonous. Juice mixed with wine lees plunges birds into lethargy; in powdered form it is useful against cancerous wounds.

Hemp (also known as marijuana, cannabis, weed, grass, hashish and pot) (*Cannabis sativa*). – ♄. Indian hemp yields a fatty extract which is the famous hashish. This ointment, smoked or ingested, gives ecstasies little known in the West, but which some Muslim, Buddhist and Taoist sects in the West use in well–measured doses in the study of psychurgy.[11] See the books by Baudelaire, Guaita, Bosc and Matgioi. (See *Hashish* in the *Esoteric Glossary*).

Hemp, seeds of. – Rheumatism, blennorrhagia (interior).

Henbane (also known as black henbane and stinking nightshade). (*Hyoscyamus niger*). – Hot and dry. ♈ or ♐ or ♑, ♄, ♃, is collected when ♄ is at ♏ or ♈. The decoction of its bark cures toothache, its root or seed, applied on pustules, dries them, even prevents them, as well as colic, if you carry it with you. Applied in-

---

10 Botanical term. Having a tongue in the middle of its leaves. Name of the Butcher's broom (*Ruscus hypoglossum*), the root of which is used like that of the small holly, a species of the same genus.

11 The action of man on the world of human souls. Psychurgy literally means: "action of the soul" (from the Greek *psuché*, "soul", and *ergon*, "work").

ternally, in its natural state, it provokes nervous attacks; it can be worked in such a way as to cause death, even at a distance. The whole plant, carried in the body, makes one friendly, the root is good against gout, the juice is good against liver pain, mixed with the blood of a young hare and put on its skin, all the hares in the vicinity will gather. Poultices of this plant are very good for all chest diseases. The smoke of its seeds provokes anger.

Herbs. – To stop nosebleeds, pick up with your left hand and without looking, a handful of herbs at random, saying: "I am from Noah, grass that has not been planted or sown, do what God has commanded you". You should place this herb under your nostrils and the blood will stop immediately. For greater efficacy, the herb should be gathered by moonlight (Vosges).

Holly (also known as common holly, English holly, European holly, holm and silver bush) (*Ilex aquifolium*). – ♄ ♂. If a person with fever rubs himself with the first holly bush he comes across, he will be cured, almost immediately. The infusion is sudorific.

Hops (also known as common hop) (*Humulus lupulus*). – ♄ ☽. Its root is an energetic blood purifier; flowers are a mild restorative.

Horehound (also known as white horehound and common horehound) (*Marrubium vulgare*). – Hot and dry. Harvested in early April or under ♍. Stomach emmenagogue.

Hornbeam (also known as ironwood and musclewood) (*Carpinus betulus*). – ☉, ♃. Good for making magic wands, divination and magnetic therapy.

Horned Cumin (*Hypecoum procumbens*). – Dry and moderately warm. ♍ o ♒; ♄. The berries are vermifuge; the oil from the seeds is anti-rheumatic, taken in very small quantities; pigeons like it very much, especially sprinkled with brine. The juice of the leaves kills flies (Alexis Piémontois).

Horse chestnut (also called buckeye, conker tree and Spanish chestnut) (*Aesculus hippocastanum*). – Its bark is febrifuge.

Horseradish (*Armoracia rusticana*). – ♐, ♂. Antiscorbutic, diuretic.

Hound's-tongue (also known as hound's-tooth, dog's tongue, gypsy flower and –for its smell– rats and mice) (*Cynoglossum officinale*). – Warm and dry, ♑; worn on top, it breaks down prejudices and enmities and reconciles sympathies.

HOUSELEEK (also known as sengreen and hens-and-chickens) (*Sempervivum tectorum*). – ♀ in ♍. It is eaten to break the "tying of the aglet"[12] (J.–B. Thiers). Crushed with barley flour and oil, it makes skin ailments and burns disappear.

HYACINTH (an ornamental bulbous plant of the genus *Hyacinthus*). – ☉ in ♀. Procures the friendship of great ladies. – Root juice prevents the development of the hair system and delays puberty. – Cooked root cures testicular tumours.

HYSSOP (*Hyssopus officinalis*). – In ♌. Tonic, drives away residual humours. Collected by hand, it is good for the eyes.

INDIAN SANDALWOOD (also called sandalwood and white sandalwood) (*Santalum album*). ☾. Moon scent; the oil purifies toxic viruses from the blood.

INDIAN SNAKEROOT (also known as devil pepper and serpentine wood) (*Rauvolfia serpentina*). – ♒; ☿. Dedicated to Saturn. Good against asthma; put on the head, prevents sleep; see **NETTLE**.

IRIS (Iris refers to plants of the genus *Iris* and other similar genera of the family *Iridaceae*). – ♀ in ♎; emblem of peace.

ITALIAN WOODBINE (also called Italian honeysuckle and perfoliate honeysuckle) (*Lonicera caprifolium*). – Dedicated to St. Peter.

IVY, COMMON (also known as English ivy and European ivy) (*Hedera helix*). – Cold and dry; ♉ or ♐; consecrated to Mercury, used to weave the crown of Bacchus; prevents drunkenness. Against sore throat and bad breath: Take twenty ivy leaves and put them in a small pot with old wine and a little salt. Boil everything to taste and then gargle with the liquid as hot as possible; the leaves also cure the consequences of drunkenness. Fumigating ivy kills bats. In Montenegro it is used to decorate the door on Christmas Eve and thus protects the house all year round. In Germany, the first time a cow is milked in spring, it is milked through a wreath of this plant.

---

12 A spell that was believed to have the power to prevent the consummation of marriage, rendering the man impotent (in French Nouer l'aiguillette).

Japanese raisin tree (also known as oriental raisin tree) (*Hovenia dulcis*). – ♄. Powder is specific, for haemorrhages and dysentery.

Japanese star anise (also called aniseed tree, and sacred anise tree) (*Illicium anisatum*). – Carminative.

Jimson weed (also known as thorn apple, stinkweed, mad apple and devil's snare) (*Datura stramonium*). – ♄ and ☽. Soporific; narcotic; used by magicians; removes bad fluids.

Juniper (*Juniperus communis*). – ♀ in ♓. A branch of this tree makes snakes flee because it bears in various ways the sign of the Trinity. Its triangular seeds, as well as its berries, called Ebel by Rullandus, or Harmat, are good against dropsy, plague, poison, colic, cough, asthma, scabies and gout. Its decoction with elderflower decoction is good against haemorrhoids. Its extract, or honey, is excellent against asthma. Its seed cures the possessed. The berries, burnt in a room, purify it. The oil from its wood (miera) is good against rheumatism and skin diseases. The great juniper gives a resin called Sandaraque.

Knotgrass (also called common knotgrass, prostrate knotweed, birdweed, pigweed nad lowgrass) (*Polygonum aviculare*). – ♃ o ☉. If the leaves are applied to a bruised wound and placed in a moist place, healing occurs magnetically. It cures heart and stomach pain. Its infusion is good for love, against lung congestion and melancholy; the root carried on oneself cures eye pain. Astringent.

Kousa (also called kousa dogwood, Chinese dogwood, Korean dogwood and Japanese dogwood) (*Cornus kousa*). – ☉. Sacred herb of the Hindus. – It is indispensable for all acts of religious and ascetic life. It has powerful magnetic properties. It is a universal vehicle.

LAMB'S EAR (also known as woolly hedgenettle) (*Stachys byzantina, syn. Stachys lanata*). – Picked when ♂ is in good appearance with ♃. Scarring.

LARKSPUR (also known as forking larkspur, rocket-larkspur, royal knight's-spur and field larkspur) (*Consolida regalis*). – Hot and dry, ♀ in ♐ or ♒. Collected after the full moon that ends the canicular days. Dedicated to Juno or Lucina; its powder is vulnerary and anti-hemorrhoidal; Paracelsus uses it a lot with **BUCK-WHEAT** and **ALOE**, **ST. JOHN'S WORT**, **BAY TREE** oil, etc. To collect the bedbugs alive and without touching them, put a few leaves of this plant under the bed-side table, all the bedbugs will gather there. The decoction as a compress is good against leucoma; the root against the flow of blood.

LAVENDER (also known as true lavender, garden lavender, common lavender and narrow-leaved lavender) (*Lavandula angustifolia*). – Warm and dry, ♌. It is collected when ☉ is ♓ and ☾ is ♋. Its fumigation drives away evil spirits. In wine, it awakens the lymph; its oil is useful for convulsions.

LEEK (*Allium ampeloprasum var. porrum*). – ♓ or ♏, ♂ and ☾. Mixed with a sympathetic food, it is diuretic and causes menstruation. Its seed recovers spoiled vinegar; cooked, it is excellent for pleurisy.

LEMON BALM (also known as balm, common balm and balm mint) (*Melissa officinalis*). – ☉ and ♃. Inspired women in ancient temples used it as an energising drink; lemon balm water mixed with male artemisia (*Artemisia abrotanum*) and emerald,[13] prepared is good for labour pains (Paracelsus), helps the expulsion of the placenta and membranes. The flowers are antispasmodic; cordial, hepatic and ophthalmic. Carried on the person, it makes it friendly: tied to the neck of an ox, it makes it follow you everywhere.

LEMON TREE (*Citrus × limon*). – ♃. The lemon has the signature of ♓ and ☉. The juice of the second bark of this wood is a very suitable poultice for curing inflammation of the eyes. The fruit is a remedy against the consequences of drunkenness and narcotic poisoning.

---

13 Alchemy term. Emerald of the philosophers, the dew of March and the dew of September.

LESSER CELANDINE (also known as figwort and pilewort because of thickening of the roots reminiscent of haemorrhoids) (*Ficaria verna*). – Warm and moderately dry; ♐; ☉: the root is warm and dry, has the sign of ♈, is good against gangrene. Picked at the right time, it is used effectively in all magical operations to ensure the success of enterprises, especially in processes. If it is put on the head of a sick person, he will sing if he is to die and weep if he is to live. – Pick the one that grows in the ruins.

LETTUCE (*Lactuca sativa*). – ♓ and ☾. Soporific, increases breast milk.

LICHEN. – Emblem of solitude.

LICORICE (also known as liquorice) (*Glycyrrhiza glabra*). – Diuretic, soothing.

LILY OF THE VALLEY (also known as may bells, Our Lady's tears and Mary's tears) (*Convallaria majalis*). – Externally: scrofula; internally: hysteria.

LILY (the species of *Lilium*, commonly called lilies, are a genus of about 110 members of the family *Liliaceae*). – Cold and dry, ♉, ♃ or ♀; better ☾. Its bulb is warm and dry, signed by ♈. Its flower is the image of the creation of the universe, of pre-formation, of the action of primitive fire on the mother water; Gabriel carries it in his message to Mary; it is the emblem of chastity; in the Middle Ages its pollen was believed to be diuretic for women who did not keep chastity. It is good against burns; it whitens the complexion; the tip of the root, crushed in rancid fat, cures leprosy (St. Hildegard). The root, collected in conjunction with ♀ and ☾ in ♉ or ♎, and suspended from the neck reconciles love; its distilled water reduces labour pains, eye pains and stomach pains; the bulb, crushed and boiled with breadcrumbs, causes abscesses to ripen and burst in a short time. – Perfumes can be made with this plant that make the room in which they are burnt suitable for astral manifestations. If a woman in labour eats two pieces of the root, she will get rid of the placenta, the membranes and the dead foetus.

LIME TREE (the European species are known as linden, the North American ones, basswood; in Britain and Ireland they are usually called lime trees or lime bushes) (genus *Tilia*, the typical species is *Tilia europaea*). – Moderately hot and humid, ☾ in ♎; the flower is signed by ♐. The infusion is calming (menstruation, epilepsy, colic); then it should be done when the ☾ is in ♓.

LITTLE BURDOCK (also known as burdock, lesser burdock, louse-bur, common burdock, button-bur, cuckoo-button, and wild rhubarb) (*Arctium minus*). – Cold and dry. ♓ o ♒. Fumigation of its seeds has the same properties as the pollen decoction of lily flowers (Porta, Wecker). Acts on skin excretion: skin diseases, ulcers, gout, syphilis.

LOTUS (French lotus, an ambiguous vernacular name for various plants, trees, shrubs or herbs, terrestrial or aquatic, such as the Egyptian Lotus, *Nymphaea lotus* or the Sacred Lotus, *Nelumbo nucifera*, etc.). – ☉. From the religious point of view, it has the same meaning as the lily; the Buddha presents it to Maya.

LUNGWORT (also called common lungwort, Mary's tears and Our Lady's milk drops) (*Pulmonaria officinalis*). – ☿ and ♄. Flower refreshes and dries; for external use, useful for wounds.

MADDER (also known as rose madder, common madder, dyer's madder and garden madder) (*Rubia tinctorum*). – ♃ and ♂. Cures hernias; good against dropsy, jaundice and suppression of menstruation; collected in May and June.

MALE FERN (also known as bear's paw and American aspidium) (*Dryopteris filix-mas*). – ♐, ♄, and a little ♂. The pulverised root is good against tapeworm, and this remedy, indicated by Galen, was sold at a very high price to Louis XV by Madame Nouffleur: it is also used for spells, cooked in wine, opens obstructions of the spleen, cures melancholy, provokes menstruation, prevents generation, is a symbol of humility, puts nightmares to flight, drives away lightning, hail, demons and enchantments. – A sprig of fern picked at midday on the eve of St. John's Eve wins the game (J.-B. Thiers).

MALLOW (*Mallow* is a genus of about 30 species of several hundred described, herbaceous plants of the family *Malvaceae*). – Cold and dry, ♉ or ♎. Our ancestors, fond of spicy jokes, used the smoke obtained by burning this plant to ensure the virginity of girls. – Soothing, good for all inflammations.

MANDRAKE (*Mandragora officinarum, Mandragora autumnalis*). – Cool and moderately dry; ♑; ♄ or ☾. One of the twelve plants of the Rosicrucians. It is bad; it can cause insanity unless corrected by the ☉; then it is a good narcotic. It was used by the Germanic people to make statues of the household gods they called Abrunes. Witches used it to go to the Sabbath. This root is one of the most powerful astral capacitors; and the human form that affects it always indicates very special properties and a special energy. Our friend Sisera possesses one that exactly represents a father, a mother and a son in the middle. It was used in the insane theories of certain magicians who wanted to find in it the elixir of long life or to make false teraphim.[14]

MARIJUANA. See **HEMP.**

MARJORAM (also known as sweet marjoram and pot marjoram) (*Origanum majorana*). – Warm and dry, ♈, ☉ or ☿. Harvested in early April or under ♏. The oil extracted is good for lethargy and apoplexy. Peeled and reduced to powder, it drives ants away from the place where it is put.

MARSH DOCK (*Rumex palustris*). – Depurative; against jaundice and skin diseases.

MARSH-MALLOW (also known as white-mallow) (*Althaea officinalis*). – Its etymology indicates an action that removes evil by cleansing or purging. Indeed, all parts of the plant are emollient and are used in infusions, poultices and baths against inflammations. Warm and moist; ♓ or ♎. Seed powdered and kneaded into ointment, preserves from insect bites, if rubbed on face and hands. The flower, kneaded with pork fat and turpentine and applied to the belly dissolves inflammations of the womb. The root, infused in wine, cures urine retention.

MEADOW SAFFRON (also known as autumn crocus and naked ladies) (*Colchicum autumnale*). – ♃ en ♓. Excellent remedy for gout; formed the basis of the famous Duke of Portland's powder and Dr. Husson's medicinal water. The bulb is very diuretic.

MINT (*Mentha* is a genus of herbaceous perennial plants, belonging to the family *Lamiaceae*). – Hot and dry, ♈ or ♌, ♃ or ♂. Collection after the full moon which ends the canicular days; or ☉ at ♌ with ☽ at ♏; or ☉ at ♉ with ☽ at ♓. Offering to the dead; Minthe, a naiad associated with the river Cocytus, beloved of Pluto, was transformed by Persephone (Pluto's wife) into mint.

MISTLETOE (also called oak mistletoe, druid's herb, golden bough, holy wood, the kissing bush, European mistletoe and common mistletoe) (*Viscum album*). – Cold and dry; ♉. Its infusion taken at the end of the menstrual period facilitates conception (Pliny). Dried berries, pulverised, and dissolved in a generous wine are good against epilepsy. Fresh, it facilitates childbirth. The Druids picked it with great pomp, at Christmas, at a precise astronomical hour; the berries, which

---

14 Images related to the magical rites used by those Israelites who added magical practices to the patriarchal religion. The teraphim were consulted by the Israelites for oracular answers.

at that time were saturated with the triple magnetism of the tree, the stars and the pious crowd, became powerful magnetic condensers and were used to operate marvellous cures in desperate cases. A branch hanging from a tree with a swallow's wing attracts all birds. Hawthorn mistletoe berries provide a good tincture against chest diseases. (See *Oak Mistletoe* in the *Esoteric Glossary*)

Moss (*Bryophyta* plant that forms soft mats in forests and meadows. Common name for various algae and lichens). – ♄. Its decoction makes hair grow, strengthens teeth, stops haemorrhages; that collected from moon trees, cooked in wine, is a diuretic and a sleeping pill.

Mulberry (white, *Morus alba*; black, *Morus nigra*; red: *Morus rubra*). – Cold and dry. ♑, consecrated to Mercury. Blackberries have the sign of ♃; red ones are appetisers and purgative; green ones are good for fluxions, dysentery, when spitting blood, and inflammations of the mouth.

Mullein (also known as common mullein, big taper, flannel mullein, flannel plant, great mullein, velvet dock, velvet plant and woolly mullein; in France it is known as Herbe de Saint-Fiacre) (*Verbascum thapsus*). – ♎. The emollient leaves and prayers to Saint-Fiacre relieve colic.[15] Cold and dry, ♏, especially the leaf or ♑; ♃. Soothing, emollient, vermifuge.

Mustard (this name refers to several plants, their seed and the condiment obtained from them: white mustard, *Sinapis alba* and black mustard, *Brassica nigra*). – ♂. The seed symbolises Christ and omniscience. The black one is anti-scorbutic.

Myrrh (gummy resinous exudation of the tree *Commiphora myrrha*). – ♀. This resin, according to mythology, was produced by the tears of Myrrh, the incestuous mother of Adonis. Myrrh absorbed in alcohol prolongs life (Van Helmont).

Myrtle (*Myrtus communis*). – Cold and dry; ♉, ♀. Dedicated to Venus and the Lares gods.[16] Image of Compassion. The leaves twisted into a wreath, cure

---

15 This plant appears under two similar names, but referring to two different plants, in the original text of Sédir, the first time it appears as *Bouillon blanc, verbascum ploma, Molène, bonhomme h. de saint Fiacre*, and the second time as *Molène. Herbe de Saint-Fiacre*, but both refer to the same species, the use of different names for the same plant is considered an error by botanists. We consolidate both texts under the name **Mullein**, the upper text is the one assigned by Sédir to the name *Bouillon blanc*, and the following one to the second name.

16 The Lares were tutelary deities; deceased ancestors regarded as protectors of the family. The domestic Lares were the tutelar deities of a house; household gods of the Romans.

tumours. The vapours of its infusion, inhaled through the mouth, drive away migraine. The dried fruit, pulverised and candied with egg white, applied as a poultice over the mouth and stomach, stops vomiting.

NETTLE (nettle is the common name for many plants of the genus *Urtica*, of the *Urticaceae* family; a common species is Urtica dioica, often known as common nettle or stinging nettle). – Warm and dry, ♌, ♂, emblem of lust. It is collected with ☉ in ♌ and ☽ in ♏, or ☉ in ♉ and ☽ in ♓. The odourless species softens tumours, cures gout, asthma. It should be collected when ♂ is in the East, in ♏ or ♑. Worn on the person, it gives courage; a nettle placed in the fresh urine of a sick person and left for 24 hours will indicate, if dry, that the sick person will die, if still green, that he will live. The juice mixed with that of the snake, if one rubs one's hands with it and throws the rest into the river, will make it easier to catch many fish with one's hand. The seed cooked in wine cures pleurisy and inflammation of the lungs; the crushed leaves stop gangrene; decoction of the seed cures fungal poisoning.

NORWAY MAPLE (*Acer platanoides*). – ♃. Consecrated to the genius of whoever planted it.

NUEZA or **DEVIL'S TURNIP** (*Bryonia dioica*). – ♂ in ♑. – Used in black magic.

NUTMEG TREE (*Myristica fragrans*). – Hot and dry. The flower is strongly signified by ♈. Facilitates conception. The nut itself, taken on an empty stomach, delays the intoxication of wine.

OAK (also known as common oak, pedunculate oak, European oak and English oak) (*Quercus robur*). – Cold and dry; ♉ or perhaps ♏, ♃. Emblem of strength, considered the tree of science by the druids. The oak is magnetic and attractive, tough and hard, hence black and dark. It carries past idolatry and sins in the infernal hunger of anger, within the *Turba magna*. – Bark is very astringent; renew mucous membranes; febrifuge.

OATS (also called common oat) (*Avena sativa*). – ☉, ☽. To cure scabies, roll naked in a field of oats, pluck a handful, rub the body with water from the spring, then dry on a tree or in a hedge; the scabies will gradually dry up; can also be used in hot poultices with wine against rheumatism.

OLIVE TREE (*Olea europaea*). – ♃. ☉. Dedicated to Minerva; emblem of peace. The oil is a powerful condenser of light; very useful in magical medicine. Two fingers of olive oil, taken on an empty stomach, prevent drunkenness. If one writes the word Athena on an olive leaf and sticks it on one's head, the migraine will disappear.

ONION (also known as bulb onion and common onion) (*Allium cepa*). – ♐, ♂. Aphrodisiac, diuretic and menstrual when eaten with a sympathetic. Its corrector is vinegar (♄). Against earache: boil a small onion under ashes, put it in a thin cloth with some fresh unsalted butter and apply it to the ear, as hot as possible, for one minute.

OPIUM POPPY (also known as breadseed poppy) (*Papaver somniferum*). – ♃ and ☾; emblem of laziness. The flowers are marked by ♄ in ♒. – The juice of the plant kills flies (Alexis Piémontois).

ORANGE TREE (also known as sweet orange and Valencia orange) (*Citrus sinensis*). – Emblem of chastity. Oranges cure the effects of long binges. To cure metrorrhagia, take seven oranges, boil the peel in three pints of water until reduced to one third, serve sweetened, twelve tablespoons three or four times a day.

OREGANO (also known as wild marjoram) (*Origanum vulgare*). – ♂, ♀. – Stimulant; emmenagogue; against rheumatism.

ORPINE (also known as livelong, frog's-stomach, Orphan John and witch's moneybags) (*Hylotelephium telephium*). – Healing.

OX-EYE DAISY (also known as daisies, oxeye daisy and dog daisy) (*Leucanthemum vulgare*). – ♒ and ☿. Decoction of the whole plant resolves inflammations of the mouth. – Salt resolves blockages of bile or stones. Eating a daisy cures fever.

PALM TREE (trees belonging to the family *Arecaceae*). – Sacred to Jupiter, emblem of victory, in particular mystical triumph; develops like Jupiter from the inside out.

PARSLEY (also known as garden parsley) (*Petroselinum crispum*). – ♓; ♄ and ☉. The seed is controlled by ♋; collected with ☉ in ♉ and ☾ waning, in lemonade, it is healing, good for gout and purgative; if oil is extracted from it for rubbing the navel, stone pain is relieved; when ♃ is in ♌ the ☾ and below the horizon, it cures dropsy. It restores the menstrual course if taken in infusion. or in oil (apiol: active principle of parsley seeds), it is also good against anaemia.

PEACH TREE (also known as nectarine tree) (*Prunus persica*). – ♃. Dedicated to Harpocrates. A few peaches, taken on an empty stomach, prevent the effects of drunkenness; a glass of peach leaf juice produces the same effect. Leaves pickled in vinegar with mint and alum, then applied to the navel, are an infallible vermifuge for children.

PELLITORY OF THE WALL (also known as upright pellitory and lichwort) (*Parietaria officinalis*). – or ♎, ♒; dedicated to St. Peter, the emblem of poverty. It is good for inflammatory diseases, dropsy and renal lithiasis; applying its juice in doses of 30 to 60 grams per day. As a poultice for painful tumours and infantile colic.

PENNYROYAL (also known as pennyrile, squaw mint, mosquito plant, and pudding grass) (*Mentha pulegium*). – Dedicated to Ceres. The yellow-flowered variety is purgative, good against scabies; on St. Roch's Day tufts were blessed and tied up in stables.

PEONY (also known as common peony and garden peony) (*Paeonia officinalis*). – Warm, dry and somewhat moist ☾ or ♋; ♃ or ☉, collect with ☉ and ☾ in ♋. The flower and especially the calyx are signed by ☾. Its distilled water, taken when ☾, ♂, and ♃ are in ♋; it is good for epilepsy and menstrual crises; for epilepsy in small children, it is enough to collect the first seeds that a young seedling gives, hang them around the neck of the child and give him/her a decoction; it also relieves all headaches, and childbirth pains. Protects against spells and sudden scares.

PEPPER (belongs to the genus *Piper*, one of the best known species of which is *Piper nigrum*, black pepper). – Hot and dry, ♌, ♂ or ☉. Serves as perfume.

PEPPERMINT (also known as American mint, brandy mint, lamb mint and lammint) (*Mentha piperita*). – Hot and humid; ♎.

PERIWINKLE (also known as dwarf periwinkle and lesser periwinkle) (*Vinca minor*). – Cold and dry, ♉. Distilled water magnetised in a certain way proves the fidelity of spouses. Pulverised with earthworms, it gives love to those who eat it with meat. Mixed with sulphur and thrown into a pond, it kills all fish. Thrown into a fire, it turns it bluish; given to a buffalo, it kills it immediately. Good for the throat.

PEYOTE (also known as cactus pudding, devil's root, diabolic root, dry whiskey, dumpling cactus, indian dope, mescal, mescal button, turnip cactus, whiskey cactus and white mule). – The dried leaves of a cactus, *Lophophora williamsii*, are used; the Indians of Texas and New Mexico obtain visual hallucinations by chewing this substance.

PINE TREE (tree of the genus *Pinus*, belonging to the class *Coniferae*). – ♄ in ♋; dedicated to Cybele and Pan. It is one of the oldest tree species on the planet. The pine cone is signed by ♈; it is used to reveal a person's mystical number. To do this, first thing in the morning, after having purified oneself, one should attend the sunrise in a pine forest; as soon as the solar disc has appeared on the horizon, one should start walking in as wide a circle as possible in order to be back at the starting point when the sun is fully visible; the number of pine cones one sees on the ground during this walk will be one's mystical number, or the number governing the question or topic for which the consultation was made.

PLANTAIN (herbaceous perennial plants of the family *Plantaginaceae*, known as greater plantain, *Plantago major* and narrowleaf plantain, *Plantago lanceolata*). – Hot, dry and a little moist; ♈, or ♌; ☉. Collect when ☉ and ☾ are in ♋ or when ☉ is in ♓ and ☾ in ♋. The roots are good against migraines and ulcers, and excess menstrual flow; the whole plant cures curses and jaundice; the leaves are pounded into poultices, which cure ulcers; the seeds pounded in wine or the leaves candied in vinegar stop dysentery. Eaten raw after dry bread and without drinking, stops dropsy; the root infused in wine is a counter-poison to opium; the water is good for the eyes.

PLUM (also known as common plum and European plum) (*Prunus domestica*). – Dry and moderately, cold ♏; the wood of this tree is ♏, ♃.

POLYPODIUM (is a genus of ferns of the order *Polypodiales*, the best known member of which is *Polypodium vulgare*, also called common polypody and polypody of the oak). – ♄; ♀ and ☽. The powder of its root is good against polyps of the nose, quartan fevers; fumigated, it drives away nightmares.

POMEGRANATE (*Punica granatum*). – ♃ in ♓. The pomegranate tree is subject to ♈. Its juice purifies the blood.

POPLAR (poplars belong to the genus *Populus*, perhaps the best known species are the black poplar, *Populus nigra* and the white poplar, *Populus alba*). – ♃; dedicated to Hercules. The white species grew on the banks of the Acheron,[17] it was, according to Homer, consecrated to the infernal gods.

POPPY, COMMON (also called corn poppy, corn rose, field poppy, Flanders poppy and red poppy) (*Papaver rhoeas*). – ☽ in ♓. Being too phlegmatic, it is good to correct it with ☉ or ☿ liquids; thus it is refreshing, anaesthetic, cures pleurisy with its juice or flower powder, and erysipelas of the head with its distilled water.

POT MARIGOLD (also known as marigolds, ruddles, common marigold and Scotch marigold) (*Calendula officinalis*). – Flowers are good for plague; leaves for scars and indurations.

PRIVET (also called wild privet, common privet and European privet) (*Ligustrum vulgare*). – Hot and dry. ♈. Can be collected under ♌.

PURSLANE (also known as purslain and pursley) (*Portulaca oleracea*). – ♋ or ♎ or ♓. It prevents the consequences of drunkenness. Fumigation of its seeds has the same virtue as lily pollen (Porta, Wecker). The juice mixed with boiled wine is the poison for henbane. The seed, crushed and eaten with honey, is good against asthma. If you put this plant in your bed, you will not have visions.

QUINCE (*Cydonia oblonga*). – Juno crowned herself with its leaves. Very astringent.

---

17 In Greek and Roman mythology, the name of a river in Hades, over which the souls of the dead were ferried by Charon; hence, a general name for the lower world.

RAMPION (also called rampion bellflower, rover bellflower and rapunzel) (*Campanula rapunculus*). – ♋ and ♍ if harvested at the end of October.

RASPBERRY (also called common red raspberry, western red raspberry and American red raspberry) (*Rubus idaeus*). – Astringent leaves for gargling; flowers in infusion for ophthalmology.

RED BEET (*Beta vulgaris var. conditiva*). – Moist and cold. ♏ or better ♐.

RED CABBAGE (*Brassica oleracea var. capitata f. rubra*). – ☽ and ♃. It is the best species. Eaten before a feast, it prevents the effects of too much wine; vulnerary, good against jaundice and bile. Its essence is a universal medicine.

RED SANDALWOOD (also called red sanders, red saunders, Rakt Chandan and saunderswood) (*Pterocarpus santalinus*). – Hot and dry, ♌. Good against haemorrhages.

RED SANDSPURRY (also known as red sand-spurrey and sand spurrey) (*Spergularia rubra*). – Grey plant, small tufts, red flowers, 5 sepals, 5 petals, 10 stamens, 3 styles; capsular flowering from April to September. In infusion with 40 grams per litre, evacuates kidney stones and calms renal colic.

REEDS (any tall broad-leafed grass growing on the margins of streams or in other wet places). – ☿. To cure dislocations of the limbs, take two reeds, put them inside each other and carry them with you; only a strong will is needed.

RESEDA (the words used by Sédir, *Réséda, Herbe de Saint-Luc*, are not enough to identify the species, only the genus of this plant: *Reseda*, of the family *Resedaceae*, which includes species as weld, dyer's rocket and bastard rocket). – ☉ and ♀. The seer Catherine Emmerich states that the evangelist Luke used it dipped in oil to make anointings or, dried, in an infusion. It has, in mysticism, a special relationship with the Virgin Mary (Catherine Emmerich), symbol of sweetness.

RHUBARB (this is the common name for about thirty species of herbaceous perennial plants of the genus *Rheum* in the family *Polygonaceae*). – ♃ and ♄. Purgative, cures jaundice.

RIVER GLADIOLUS (*Gladiolus palustris?*). – ♂ in ♋. Aphrodisiac.

ROSE OF JERICHO (also called Maryam's flower, flower of St Mary, St. Mary's flower, Mary's flower and white mustard flower) (*Anastatica hierochuntica*). – It has the same signatures than the Rose with a particular action of ♄ in ♋. If a pregnant woman puts it in water and it flowers perfectly, the woman will have a happy birth (Trad. provençales, J.-B. Thiers).

ROSE (bushes form the genus *Rosa* of the family *Rosaceae*). – Cold and dry; ♉, ☿ and ♃. The Rose is an initiatory flower, one of the twelve used by the Rosicrucians, emblem of love, patience, martyrdom, the Virgin. In syrup or infusion, it is called mucarum or mucharum; it facilitates conception if the flowers used are red. The water distilled from the flowers is good for all venereal flows and for ophthalmia; it can be used to make a perfume and a liqueur that prepares the intellectual soul for revelations from above. A seed with a mustard seed and the leg of a weasel, hung on a tree, makes it sterile; the same composition makes dead cabbages green again in a day; in a lamp, it causes hallucinations.

ROSEMARY (*Salvia rosmarinus*). – Warm and dry; ♈; ☉ or ♃ is harvested in early April or under ♍; consecrated to the lares gods. Paracelsus calls its flower Anthos. The oil of the flowers is white, transparent; aromatic and vulnerary. The water from the same flowers is the famous Queen of Hungary's Water.[18] Its flowers, boiled in white wine, in lotions, refresh the face and in gargles, perfume the breath. Good as a detersive against leprosy, syphilis and wounds.

SAFFRON (also called saffron crocus and autumn crocus) (*Crocus sativus*). – Warm and dry, ♌ or ♐, ☉. Collect when the ☉ is in ♓ and the ☽ is in ♋.

SAGE (also known as garden sage, common sage and culinary sage) (*Salvia officinalis*). – Hot and dry, ♈, ☉. Its name comes from the two Tudesque words Sol-heil. The leaves are vulnerary. The arcane[19] that can be extracted from them

---

18 Queen of Hungary's Water is an aromatic extract obtained by distilling the rosemary flower with eau-de-vie.

19 Alchemical term. Mysterious operation. By extension, a remedy whose composition is kept secret.

is reviving and regenerating. Its seed, called Ebel, in infusion, facilitates conception.

Salad burnet (also known as garden burnet, small burnet and burnet) (*Sanguisorba minor*). – Cures evil spells when tied around the neck. Its juice kills flies. Chew it in times of plague.

Sarsaparilla (also known as common smilax, rough bindweed, sarsaparille and Mediterranean smilax) (*Smilax aspera*). – The root ☿ in ♋. Its infusion is depurative, used against diseases of Venus and obesity.

Saxifrage (saxifrages are herbaceous perennial plants of the family *Saxifragaceae* belonging to the genus *Saxifraga*, tipically the *Pimpinella saxifraga*, lesser burnet). – ♋, ♎, ♒, ♄. The seeds are used, taken in the juice of the plant, to dissolve bladder stones.

Scarlet pimpernel (also known as blue-scarlet pimpernel, red pimpernel, red chickweed, poor man's barometer, poor man's weather-glass, shepherd's weather glass and shepherd's clock) (*Lysimachia arvensis*). – ♓ or ♋, ♎; if collected in late October ♏, ♃. For enteritis.

Scurvy-grass (also known as common scurvygrass and spoonwort) (*Cochlearia officinalis*). – Very tonic; good against all forms of scrofula and for gums.

Sea squill (also known as squill, sea onion, red squill, and maritime squill) (*Drimia maritima*). – For dropsy.

Self-heal (also known as heal-all, woundwort and heart-of-the-earth) (*Prunella vulgaris*). – ♃ ♂ y ☿. Heals all kinds of wounds, mainly of the mouth; if the diseased tooth is rubbed of its dried root, collected in August, until a little blood comes out, the pain ceases; the decayed tooth should then be covered with a little willow. Makes boils ripen (in wine); its ingestion is useful against haemorrhoids.

Senna (also known as Alexandrian senna) (*Senna alexandrina*). – ☉, ☽ and ♄; decoction is purgative.

Service tree (also called rowan berry and sorb tree) (*Sorbus domestica*). – Warm and humid. ♏; ♃. Romulus' javelin was made of its wood; serves against spells.

Sesame (also known as benne) (*Sesamum indicum*). – ♃. Its seeds are used by Hindus in their domestic sacrifices to the ancestral manes, or Pitris.

Shepherd's purse (also called shepherd's scrip, shepherd's sprout, lady's purse, witches' pouches, rattle pouches, pick-purse, mother's heart and clappedepouch in Ireland) (*Capsella bursa-pastoris*). – ♄. Useful for spells; stops haemorrhages and diarrhoea. Crushed in vinegar and squeezed in the palms of the hands, it is good against blennorrhagia. Held in the hand by a man, or hung around the neck by a woman, it stops the flow of blood.

Silver thistle (also known as stemless carline thistle, dwarf carline thistle and weather thistle) (*Carlina acaulis*). – If harvested at the end of October, it is subjected to ♏ and ♂. Aphrodisiac.

Silverweed (also called common silverweed, silver cinquefoil and wild tansy) (*Argentina anserina*). – Stops all flows coming from the weakness of the organs: intestines, womb, blood vessels; good against scurvy, dropsy, jaundice.

Soapwort (also known as bouncing-bet, crow soap, sopewort and bruisewort) (*Saponaria officinalis*). – ♄. Consecrated to St Peter's. Excellent for syphilis.

Sorrel (also known as spinach dock and narrow-leaved dock) (*Rumex acetosa*). – Warm and moist, ♓ or ♍. The root, cut into small slices, soaked for 4 hours in strong white vinegar, is used as a lotion against skin peeling. The seed, collected by a virgin child, prevents nocturnal pollutions. – Purifying, refreshing.

Sour cherry (also known as tart cherry and dwarf cherry) (*Prunus cerasus*). – ♃ in ♓. The fruits are purifying and refreshing, good for combating the consequences of drunkenness.

Southern maidenhair fern (also known as black maidenhair fern, maidenhair fern and venus hair fern) (*Adiantum capillus-veneris*). – Cold and dry, ♉.

Southernwood (also called lad's love and southern wormwood) (*Artemisia abrotanum*). – Hot and dry; ♎. Collect in early April or under ♍. Good for childbirth.

Speedwell (also known as heath speedwell, common gypsyweed, common speedwell and Paul's betony) (*Veronica officinalis*). – Warm and dry, ♈. Harvested after the full moon which ends the canicular days. Used to treat lung and blood disorders.

Spindle tree (also known as European spindle, prick timber, prickwood, spindleberry and common spindle) (*Euonymus europaeus*). – ♃ in ♑. Its wood is good for cleansing the liver.

SPINY RESTHARROW (also called restharrow and cammock) (*Ononis spinosa*). – ♂ and ♃. It cures pleurisy; collected under the conjunction of these two planets, in the X house, it can be used as a talisman against the dangers of war, thieves and quarrels.

SQUASH (certain varieties of squash as *Cucurbita pepo* and *Cucurbita citrullus*). – Soothing, refreshing.

ST. JOHN'S WORT (also known as perforate St John's-wort and common Saint John's wort) (*Hypericum perforatum*). – Warm, dry and somewhat moist; ☉, ♈ or ♋; collected when the ☉ and ☽ are at ♋ or ☉ at ♌ and in good appearance with ♃. It was one of the twelve plants of the Rosicrucians. If it is gathered on the day after St. John the Baptist, when that day falls on a new moon, it is hung before dawn from oak stakes in a field, then the field becomes fertile. One may be content to pick the grass on a Friday before dawn. It is used to fumigate rooms against ligature.[20] In Germany it is hostile to witches when gathered at night; on the morning of St. John's Day wreaths are plaited with it which are worn while dancing round the fire and kept as a preservative. In the Norman Bocage, gathered on the eve of St. John's Day, it destroys the evil spells that prevent cows from giving butter. In Germany, neither demons nor witches have power over those who wear them. A branch hung on the door of a house or buried under the threshold prevents a witch from entering (against hysteria, epilepsy). In southern Germany and Bohemia, it is made into a belt and thrown into a fire lit for the saint and thus protected throughout the year (Mélusine). Thrown here and there at sowing time, it preserves the field from hail. Its juice is sovereign for healing wounds; its water is sudorific, vermifugal; they make perfumes of it against the spirits that guard treasures and against obsessive demons (Raymond Lully). A twig placed in the shoe preserves from evil spirits; carried in the hand or in tincture, then infused to wash the feet, it prevents any tiredness when walking; in fumigation, it frees women from the dead fruit of their womb; boiled in wine and drunk in small and repeated doses, it prevents abortion; emmenagogue.[21]

STAVESACRE (*Delphinium staphisagria*). – ♄. Vomit, crushed with oil and used in lotions, kills lice.

---

20 Here *ligature* refers to the effect of certain curses, to which is attributed the power of suddenly suspending some function of the body, such as the consummation of marriage.
21 This plant is found under two different names in the book of Sédir, although the plant is one and the same. The first mention, to which the text of this paragraph corresponds, is under the title *Herbe de la Saint-Jean, Armoise, Hypericon, Millepertuis, a porros*; the second mention, under the title *Mille-pertuis. Herbe de la Saint-Jean*, has only the following text: It chases away tormenting spirits.

Stinking hellebore (also known as dungwort, setterwort and bear's foot) (*Helleborus foetidus*). – Its root is poisonous, it can be used as bait to catch wolves and foxes.

Stock (also called Brompton stock, common stock, hoary stock, ten-week stock and gilly-flower) (*Matthiola incana*). – ♀.

Stonecrop (also known as goldmoss stonecrop, mossy stonecrop, prick-madam and small-houseleek) (*Sedum acre*). – Vermicular, used to combat cancer and gangrene.

Strawberries (the different species of strawberries belong to a genus of creeping plants of the family *Rosaceae*). – ♃ in ♓. The fruit is soothing, good for jaundice and against stones. If the leaves are taken and used to make a belt, snakes will not harm you.

Summer savory (*Satureja hortensis*). – ☿ in ♌. The water from its leaves kills flies (Alexis Piémontois).

Sun spurge (also known as cat's milk, madwoman's milk, sun euphorbia, umbrella milkweed, wart spurge, wart weed, wartgrass and wartweed) (*Euphorbia helioscopia*). – Cold and wet; ♂, ♏. The stem, reduced to powder, is used as a perfume because of the appeal of saturnine influences; it has the sign of ♒.

Sweet Acacia (also called huisache, mimosa bush and needle bush) (*Vachellia farnesiana*). – Cold and dry, ♉ or ♏. Purging.

Sweet alyssum (also called sweet alison or alyssum) (*Lobularia maritima*). – ☉. Found on the Mediterranean coast, anti–scorbutic.

Sweet briar (also called sweetbriar rose and sweet brier or eglantine) (*Rosa rubiginosa*). – Cold and dry, ♏.

Sweet clover (also known as yellow sweet clover, yellow melilot, mellilot, common melilot and king's claver) (*Melilotus officinalis*). – Moderately warm and moist; ♒. Good for the eyes; circulates the blood.

Sweet flag (also known as calamus, flagroot, sweet cane, sweet grass, sweetroot and sweet rush) (*Acorus Calamus*). – Somewhat cold and dry, ♍, ☉. – In East Prussia, on Midsummer's Eve, it is given to the cows. In China leaves tied in bundles are placed near the bed; on the fifth day of the fifth moon to repel evil that may enter the house, branches and pieces are placed on each side of the door and windows (Mélusine).

TAMARIND (also called Indian tamarind) (*Tamarindus indica*). – ♄, ☾. The fruit is signed by ☉. An infusion of the wood of this tree in wine cures spleen pain, leprosy and toothache. The species whose fruits are sour and black and reddish, is the best, these fruits can be used for divination.

TANSY (also known as garden tansy) (*Tanacetum vulgare*). – ♋. Bitter, aromatic and antispasmodic; good against nervous diseases; vermifuge.

TEA (infusion of the leaves and buds of the tea plant: *Camellia sinensis*). – ☿. Its infusion was once used by Japanese Buddhists as a magically influenced drink to strengthen their community.

THYME (*Thymus vulgaris*). – Hot and dry, ♌. ☉; collected when the ☉ is at ♓ and the ☾ is at ♋; emblem of activity. In infusions, for sick children; and used as an infusion for decayed teeth, and against whooping cough.

TINDER. – The agaric oak fungus.

TOBACCO (a psychotropic product made from the dried leaves of the common tobacco plant: *Nicotiana tabacum*). – ☾. Distillation gives a potent emetic, and an astringent liquor good for skin complaints. Smoked in a pipe, it predisposes to calmness and can become a support for contemplation.

TORMENTIL (also known as septfoil) (*Potentilla erecta*). – Cold and dry, ♉ or ♏; ♂; counter-poison.

TURNIP (*Brassica rapa subsp. rapa*). – ☽ in ♑. – Cooked under ashes, applied behind the ear, relieves toothache.

USNEA (a genus of lichens of the family *Parmeliaceae*, typical species are *Usnea barbata* and *Usnea filipendula*, usually called old man's beard and beard lichen).

– ♄. ☽. A kind of fungus or mould that grows on the bones of abandoned corpses. Paracelsus collected the fungi he found on the skulls of hanged men and made powerful ointments from them.

VALERIAN (also known as garden valerian) (*Valeriana officinalis*). – Cold and dry, ♉, ☿. Valeriana phu 'Aurea' is the best, for use of its root (♄) against asthma, dropsy and infections. – When presented to a hypnotised subject, it is known to make him crawl on all fours, meow and scratch; the plant is used together with the prayer to St. George for the cure of nervous diseases. In infusion, it facilitates conception.

VERVAIN (also known as common vervena) (*Verbena officinalis*). – Warm and moderately moist, ♎, ☉, or better ☿; plant of the Rosicrucians; good for divination; used to make an irresistible love potion. Water distilled from the plant is good against anaemia of the optic nerve; if distillation is carried further, a liquor is obtained which, taken in homeopathic doses, is good against tuberculosis and for dissolving blood clots in the veins. – The root cures scrofula, ulcers and abrasions. Planted, following certain rituals, in a field or near a house, it increases its prosperity. If four leaves of it are put in wine and sprinkled in a feasting hall, all the guests will rejoice. If, holding it in your hand, you ask a sick person about his health, if he replies that he is better, he will be cured, otherwise he will die. Its leaves are used against rabies, in infusion and as a poultice. The seed mixed with one-year-old peony seed cures epilepsy. It is collected at the rising of the Dog constellation, when the ☉ and ☽ are below the horizon.

VINE (also known as grape vine) (*Vitis vinifera*). – Leaf juice cures dysentery, haemorrhages and vomiting. Grape seeds, roasted, pulverised and applied to the stomach in poultices, cure dysentery. The leaves and filaments, crushed in poultices and applied to the stomach, cure women who have recently become pregnant and are suffering from disordered hunger.

VIOLET (also known as wood violet and sweet violet) (*Viola odorata*). – Cold and dry, ☿, ♃ or ♉. Pectoral and cordial.

VITEX (also called chaste tree or chastetree, chasteberry, Abraham's balm, lilac chastetree and monk's pepper) (*Vitex agnus-castus*). – ♄ in ♋. The seeds, in infusion, are used in venereal diseases. Paracelsus calls its flowers zatanca, zuccar or zuccaiar. Its soothing properties were already known to the Athenians, who put this plant in their beds during the feasts of Ceres to preserve their continence.

WALL GERMANDER (*Teucrium chamaedrys*). – Cold and dry, ♉, ♂ and ♃. Purgative, anti–inflammatory and relaxing, diuretic, sudorific; applied externally, stops haemorrhoid pain and inflammation.

WALNUT (also known as Persian walnut, English walnut, Carpathian walnut, Madeira walnut, or especially in Great Britain, common walnut) (*Juglans regia*). – ☽ in ♐. The nut is signed by ♐. The bark of the root is a counter-poison and an emetic; it cures inflammations of the mouth. The decoction of the leaves taken at the dose of one cup in the morning and evening, is excellent against scrofula, skin eruptions and swellings. It is necessary to continue the diet for a long time. This decoction is also the basis of a method of curing syphilis, but requires a patient with a very energetic vitality. The smell of the leaves attracts fleas.

WATER LILY (genus of aquatic plants used as a type for the *Nymphaaceae* family, where we can distinguish: the white water lily, *Nymphaea alba*, also called water lily, and the yellow water lily, *Nuphar lutea*). – Cold and wet; ♓, ☽ and ♀; emblem of charity; collected in June and July, cures migraines, dizziness; mixed with a ♄ plant, cures blennorrhagia; stops the movements of the flesh. Its root stops white and red flushing. Collected under favourable influences of ☽ and ♄; it can become a safe anti-aphrodisiac drink.

WATER MINT (also known as marsh mint and watermint) (*Mentha aquatica*). – Hot and dry; ♈.

WATERCRESS (also called yellowcress) (*Nasturtium officinale*). – Cold and dry; ♉. Depurative, desiccant, good for ringworm and scabies.

WAYFARING-TREE (also known as wayfarer) (*Viburnum lantana*). – ☿. Leaves in wine decoction cure epilepsy.

WELSH ONION (also called bunching onion, long green onion, Japanese bunching onion, and spring onion) (*Allium fistulosum*). – ♂ in ♍. In decoction it is good against epilepsy in small children and against all thick and sticky phlegm.

WEST INDIAN SANDALWOOD (also called Indies sandalwood) (*Amyris balsamifera*). – ☉. Used for perfumes.

WHEAT (also called common wheat and bread wheat) (*Triticum aestivum*). ☉ in ♍. – Grains of wheat, roasted in their ears, in the fires of St. John's Day, which we celebrated in our field on June 24. Cures toothache and preserves from boils.

WILD ANISE. – Warm and moist, ♎. Same properties as **ANISE**, slightly less tonic.

WILD BASIL (also called cushion calamint) (*Clinopodium vulgare*). – Hot and dry. ♈. If you put a whole plant under a plate of meat, no woman will touch it. Worn on the person, it prevents all infernal vision (Apuleius).

WILD PANSY (also known as Johnny jump up, heartsease, heart's ease, heart's delight, tickle-my-fancy, three faces in a hood and love-in-idleness) (*Viola tricolor*). – Depurative; good for infantile impetigo.

WILD VALERIAN. – It has the same virtues than **VALERIAN**.

WILLOW (willows are deciduous trees and shrubs of the genus *Salix* in the family *Salicaceae*). – ♄ in ♋; the leaves are marked ♐. The seeds and the oil extracted from them are anti-aphrodisiac, astringent, vermifuge; it was used by the ancient Germans for rhabdomancy; and by sorcerers as a divining rod to discover treasures; it prevents, if carried, infernal visions.

WINTER ACONITE (also called winter hellebore, winter wolf's bane) (*Heranthis hyemalis*). – Caustic, dangerous, emblem of slander.

WINTER-CRESS (also known as bittercress, herb barbara, rocketcress, yellow rocketcress, winter rocket, yellow rocket, and wound rocket) (*Barbarea vulgaris*). – ☉. Cruciferous, antiscorbutic and pectoral.

WOLF'S BANE (also called leopard's bane, mountain tobacco and mountain arnica) (*Arnica montana*). – ☉. One of the twelve plants of the Rosicrucians; base of the vulneraries; can poison.

WOOD AVENS (also known as colewort, herb bonet, herb Bennet and St. Benedict's herb) (*Geum urbanum*). – Its root in wine is an excellent febrifuge.

Wood sorrel (also known as common wood sorrel) (*Oxalis acetosella*). – ☿. Collected with its flowers, the essence is good, for internal use, against epilepsy and poisoning; it is also diuretic. In mysticism, it is the emblem of the Trinity. The four-leaf clover makes one lucky in gambling. It presages bad weather by leaning towards the earth with a stronger scent than usual; smoked, it relieves asthma.

Wormwood (also called grand wormwood, absinthe, absinthium, absinthe wormwood, mugwort, wermout, wermud, wormit and wormod) (*Artemisia absinthium*). – ♂ and ♑. Lower astral receptacle; it is in a way the hashish of the West; it can be used for certain experiments when its flowering tops are prepared in purity. Vermifuge, febrifuge.

Yarrow (also known as nose-bleed, milfoil and thousand-leaf) (*Achillea millefolium*). – Warm, dry, and a little moist. ♈. Picked when the ☉ and ☽ are at ♋. Stops bleeding; good for uterus and toothache.

Yellow horned poppy (also known as yellow hornpoppy and sea-poppy) (*Glaucium flavum*). – Cold and wet; ♓.

Appendixes

Bibliography

A. Rambosson — *Histoire et Légendes des plantes*, Paris 1887.

Bonnet, C. — *Contemplation de la Nature.* — Amsterdam, 1770.

Bourru and **Burot.** — *La suggestion mentale et l'action à distances des substances toxiques et médicamenteuses avec fig.*

Candolle, A.P., Dr. - *Essai sur les propriétés médicales des plantes comp. avec leurs formes extérieures et leur classification naturelle,* 1816.

Du Prel - *Die Pflanzen und der Magnetitismus. In Uber Land und Meer,* 1886-87.
 — *Das forcierte Pflanzenwachstum und der Pflanzenphonix in Uber Land und Meer.* 1887-88.

Ern. Bosc — *Traité théorique et pratique du Haschich et autres substances psychiques,* Paris, 1895, (Chap. VII).

Fermond — *Essai de phytomorphie, ou étude des causes qui déterminent lés principales formes végétales,* Paris, Germer- Baillière, 1864-1868, 2 vol.
 - *Phytogênie ou théorie mécanique de ta végétation,* Paris, 1867.
 — Études comparées des feuilles, dans les trots grands embranchements végétaux, Paris, 1864.
 — Études sur la symétrie, considérée dans les trois règnes de la Nature. Paris, 1855.

FERRIÈRE, E. — *Les plantes médicinales de la Bourgogne.* Paris 1892.

FUCHSIUS, LEONHART — *Hist. des plantes, avec les noms grecs, latins et français.* Paris, 1549.

FUMOUZE, A. – *De la cantharide officinale.* Paris, 1867.

GENLIS, DE – *La Botanique historique et littéraire,* Paris 1810.

H. DURVILLE — *Physique Magnétique,* Paris, 1896.

LANESSAN — *Introduction a la Botanique, Le Sapin.* Paris, 1890, 2nd ed.

LEMERY – *Pharmacopée universelle, etc,* Amsterdam, 1784.
   – *Dictionnaire universel des drogues.*

LOUGET — *Mouvement circulatoire de la matière dans les trois règnes,* Paris, 1874.

LUYS, DR.. — *Les Émotions dans l'État hypnotique et l'action à distance des substances toxiques et médicamenteuses avec fig.* Paris.

MAURIN, E.S. — *Formulaire de l'herboristerie.* Paris, 1888.

RAYMOND, EMMELINE – *L'esprit des fleurs; symbolisme, Science.* Paris, 1884.

RODIN, H. — *Les Plantes médicinales usuelles, des champs, jardins et forêts. Description et usages des plantes comestibles, suspectes, vénéneuses employées dans la médecine, dans l'industrie et dans l'économie domestique,* Paris.

SAFFRAY, DR.. – *Les remèdes des champs, herborisations pratiques,* Paris, Hachette, 2 vol.

SAPORLA, DE and **MARION** – *L'Évolution du règne végétal. I. Les Cryptogames,* 1881.
   – *L'Évolution du règne végétal. II. Les phanérogames,* Paris, 1885.

SCHRODER – *Pharmacopée raisonnée,* Lyon, 1698.

SPHINX, LE – Articles from fascicles of January and February 1887 and August 1888.

TROUESSART, E. — *Les microbes, les ferments et les moisissures,* Paris, 1861.

UN VEGETARIANO – *Petits remèdes, seconde série,* Paris, Carré, 1889.

ESOTERIC WORKS

BERKEYLEY, DR. GEORGE – *Recherches sur les vertus de l'eau de goudron; où l'on a joint des Réflexions Philosophiques sur divers autres Sujets.* Amsterdam, Pierre Mortier, 1745.

BAUDERON — *La Pharmacopée a laquelle outre les corrections et augmentations de toutes tes précédentes éditions, sont ajoutées de nouveau les remarques, corrections et compositions curieuses et nécessaires aux médecins, apothicaires, chirurgiens et autres,* by **FRANÇOIS VERMY**, master apothecary in medicine at the University of Montpellier. Lyon. 1663.

BOEHME, JACOB — *Soemmlliche Werke, passim.*

CHARAS, MOYSE - *Pharmacopée royale galénique et chymique.* Paris, 1676.

CRYSÈS, H. - *Nouveau Langage symbolique des plantes,* Paris, 1891.

CULPEPER - *English physician and Complete Herbal with additional herbs, with a display of their medicinal and occult properties.* 1789.

FAYOL, J.B. — *L'Harmonie céleste découvrant les diverses dispositions de la Nature...* Paris, 1672.

GUBERNATIS, DE, A. - *Mythologie des plantes,* Paris.

HEUCHEUR, M.J.H. — *Magic plants, being a translation of a curious tract entitled de Vegetalibus Magicis.* Edmund Goldsmid, 1886.

KORNMANN, H. - *Templum naturæ historicum in quo de Natura et miraculis quatuor elementorum, etc,* - Darmstadt, 1611.

LENGLET, MORTIER and **VANDAMME, D.** - *Nouvelles et véritables étymologies médicales tirées du Gaulois.* Paris and Quesnoy, 1857.

LEVIN, LEMNE - *Les secrets Miracles de Nature et enseignements de plusieurs choses par raison probables et artistes conjectures expliquet en deux livres,* por **ANTONIO DUPINET**, Lyon, 1566.
— *Les occultes merveilles et secrets de Nature avec plusieurs enseignements dés choses diverses tant par raison probable que par conjecture artificielle: exposés en deux livres.* Paris, 1567, 1574.

MACER FLORIDUS — *De Viribus herbarum,* 1845.

NYNAULD, JEAN DE — *De la Lycanthropie, transformation et extase des Sorciers, où les astuces du Diable sont mises tellement en évidence, qu'il est presque impossible, voire aux plus ignorants, de se laisser dorénavant séduire: Avec la Réfutation des Arguments contraires que **Bodin** allègue au 6° cap. du II° livre de sa Demonomanie, pour soutenir la réalité de ce ceste pretenduë transformation d'hommes en bestes.* Paris, Nicolas Rousset, 1615.

PARACELSO, English trans. by **JOHN HESTER** - *Secrets of physic and philosophy... the true and perfect order to distill of draw forth the oyles of herbes, etc...* Londres, 1633.

PERNÉTY, A.J. — *Dictionnaire mytho-hermétique*, etc…, Paris, 1758.

PLINIO – *Hist. Nat.* T. XXIV, XXV; *passim.*

PORTA, BAPT. — *Phylognomonica, octo llbris contenta; in quibus nova, facilli-maqne affertur methodus,* qua plantarum animalium, metallorum; rerum denique omnium ex prima *extimæ faciet inspectione quiuis abditas vires assequatur,* etc. Rothomagi, I. Berthelin, 1650, with an alphabetic index, Francofurti, 1561.

PORTA, J.B. - *La Magie naturelle qui est les secrets miracles de nature, mise en quatre livres…* Lyon, 1565.

STORCK, ANTONI — *Medici Viennensis et in Nosocomio civico Pazmariano, Physiet ordinarii libellus, quo* de monstratur Cicutam non solum usu interno tutissime exhiberi, sed et esse simul remedium valde utile in multis morbis qui hucusque curatu impossibiles dicebantur. Viena, 1760.
Translated in 1761, under the title of *Dissertation sur l'Usage de la Ciguë,* — Paris.
- *Libellus secundus, quo* confirmatur cicutam non solum usu interno tutissime exhiberi, sed et esse *simul remedium valde utile in multis morbis qui hucusque curatu impossibiles dicebantur.* Viena, 1761.
- *Supplementum necessarium de cicuta, ubi simul jungitur cicutæ imago oere excusa.* Viena, 1761; with a copper plate.
Translated into French under the title of: *Observations nouvelles sur l'usage de la Ciguë,… ou seconde partie et supplément nécessaire;… auxquels on a joints l'histoire de l'usage interne de la ciguë, la figure de cette plante et les cures opérées et publiées en France jusqu'à ce jour,* Paris, Didot-le-Jeune, 1762.

UNGER, F. — *Die Pflanze als Zaubermittel.* Viena, 1859.

VALLEMONT, DE – *Curiosités dé la Nature et de l'art sur la végétation ou l'agriculture et le jardinage dans leur perfection: où l'on voit le secret de la multiplication du blé, de nouvelles découvertes,* etc. Bruselas, 1734.

WECKER, J.J. - *Les secrets et merveilles de nature, recueillis de divers Autheurs et divisez en XVII livres,* Rouen, 1680.

X - *Idée de jardin du monde,* by **THOMAS THOMASEV**, médico de Rávena, 1648.

X - *Recueil de divers secrets,* 160 pages manuscript. *Recettes de médecine, droguerie, chimie, pharmacie, etc. Oeuvre inédite avec quelques pièces anc. impra-joutées.*

X — *Livre xénodocal, c'est-à-dire hospitalier ou lieu de pauvre séjour, utile et né-cessaire à tous chirurgiens,* par T. Guillaumet, Lyon, P. Rigaud, 1611. *De la vertu des plantes médicales, chirurgicales, vulnéraires, etc.*

X. — *Le messager de la vérité, contenant la composition et propriété d'un remède spécifique pour toutes sortes de maux,la vertu que l'on trouve dans les végé-taux, minéraux, sels,* etc.. Ausburgo, 1723.

X. — *Traité des signatures on vraye et vive anatomie du grand et du petit monde.*

Esoteric Glossary

This Esoteric Glossary was mostly taken from Stanislas de Guaita, *Le Temple de Satan: Inventaire de l'arsenal du sorcier.*[1]

A

ADRAMELECH. – Syrian idol; the Middle Ages made him a devil. – See ch. I.

AGGARATH. – One of the wives of Sammael, in the Pneumatics of the Talmudists.

AIGUILLETTE. – It is, in the pictorial language of Sorcery, the name of the *Phallus* that is to be paralysed, to this end to prevent the young spouses from fulfilling their conjugal duty. This is called *nouer l'aiguillette*[2] (see **TYING OF THE AGLET**).

ALBERT LE GRAND (ALBERT THE GREAT). – From the works of this theologian, bishop of Regensburg (1196-1280), fragments have been extracted from which two grimoires (see this word), even more stupid than famous, have been composed:

---

1   Published in English as *The Temple of Satan*, Ouroboros Publishing, 2020.

2   A spell that was believed to have the power to prevent the consummation of the marriage. This is indeed an old impotence spell. The counter-spell was *dénouer l'aiguillette*.

135

1° *Le Grand-Albert* (The Grand-Albert) (or *the admirable secrets of Albert the Great*) was printed many times, in the formats of in-12, in-18 and in-24. – It is divided into four books: the first deals extensively with the mysteries of animal generation, conception and seed; the second deals with the virtues attributed to plants, stones, animals, astrology and the wonders of the world; the third offers our meditations a treatise on the virtues of droppings and excrement, the properties of several unfortunate insects, and ends with a rich collection of so-called natural secrets; the fourth book is a banal treatise on *Physiognomy* and also concludes with a list of recipes. – One of the best French editions is that of *Lyon*, 1775, in-18 with figures.

2° Even more extravagant, the *Petite Albert* (Little Albert) (or the solid treasure of the) contains black magic formulas which are impertinent and baroque, but which are even more successful on the lips of our shepherds and village sorcerers; they have put all their confidence in this lampoon, which is for them the Alpha and Omega of kabbalistic science, and if they have any natural disposition, faith crowns them sorcerers. – See preferably the edition of *Lyon*, 6516, in-18, "enriched with mysterious figures and the way to make them".

Under the title of *Albert-Moderne* (Modern Albert), collections of scientific recipes have been published, with the laudable aim of modifying the prevailing ideas among the rural populations, and of substituting for the superstitious formulas dear to them some notions of positive science. Nevertheless, the incorrigible shepherd always comes back to his solid treasure.

ALMANACH DU DIABLE (DEVIL'S ALMANAC). – Semi-prophetic and semi-facétieuse publication, directed against the Jansenists, during the reign of Louis XV. Some of the predictions contained in this work may have seemed a little reckless to the authorities, who diligently removed the copies they were able to seize. As a result, the two *Almanacs of the Devil* for the years 1737 and 1738 (in the Underworld, in-24), became rare and climbed quite high in book sales.

AMULETS. – The Amulet is an object of superstitious devotion, which people carry on themselves to protect them from some misfortune, to ward off some accident or to escape some epidemic.

The Amulet is protective, a shield; it is attributed a passive and preventive virtue; this is how the Amulet differs from the Talisman (see this word), which is commonly believed to have active and acquisitive properties.

Amulets have infinite variations: from the living toad carried in a horn box as guarantee against bewitchment, to the *Agnus Dei*, to the blessed medals, scapulars and other pious objects, whose use the Church authorises and even advises.

Mascots and other *Lucky charms*, which have been so fashionable in recent years, are magical objects of a bastard nature, between the Amulet and the Talisman.

ANDRODAMAS. – A sort of fabulous magnet, which has the property of attracting silver, iron and bronze.

ANDROID. – This was the name given to certain metal statuettes, masterpieces of mechanics, to which the property of thinking, speaking and moving was attributed. All automatically.

Albert le Grand was considered to have made an *Android* who reasoned metaphysically with unfailing rigour. As this quibbling automaton accumulated syllogisms on dilemmas inexhaustibly, Saint Thomas Aquinas, weary and impatient with his deafening dialectic, smashed it to pieces with a blow of his stick.

Some sorcerers went about it in other ways to obtain an Android, or rather a *Homunculus*. – Christian excerpts this amazing recipe from a handwritten grimoire: "Take a black hen's egg and squeeze out a quantity of mucus equal to the volume of a large bean. Replace this mucus with *sperma viri*, and fill the crack in the egg with a little virgin parchment, slightly moistened. Then put your egg in a layer of manure on the first day of the moon of March, which you will know from the table of pacts. After thirty days of incubation, a small monster with some semblance of human form will emerge from the egg. You will keep it hidden in a secret place and feed it with aspic seed and earthworms. As long as it lives, you will be happy in everything." (Christian, *Histoire de la Magie* (History of Magic), p. 450-451).

And this is how the odious marries with the ridiculous. – (See the word *Mandrake*.)

ANTICHRIST. – Incarnation of the diabolic Word, as opposed to the divine Word in Jesus Christ.

APPLE. – The sorcerers, wishing to go to the Sabbath, greased their whole body with a certain ointment based on narcotic drugs: then the Devil appeared to them at "midnight", and took them to the "place" of these assemblies.

ARCANUM. – Alchemical term. Mysterious operation. By extension, a remedy whose composition is kept secret.

ASTROLABE. – This is the instrument used by Astrologers to determine the state of Heaven on the day and at the hour desired, and to draw up the *Genethic Theme* of which the *Horoscope* is the commentary.

The *Astrology* of the ancient sanctuaries was a real and profound science; unfortunately, it has become depraved by being vulgarised, to the point of becoming unrecognisable.

Judicial Astrology,[3] which was so honoured in the Middle Ages and which still has fervent supporters today, is one of the most illusory and ridiculous things imaginable. – See Fabre d'Olivet's excellent essay on the Astrology of the Ancients; it is a page as deep as it is substantial: *Vers dorés de Pythagore* (Golden Verses of Pythagoras), Paris, 1813, 1 vol. in-8 (pp. 269-278, sixteenth review).

ATTRACTIVE PLANT (by *Van Helmont*). – On page 708 of the complete works of this spagyric theosophist (published in Frankfurt MDC LXXXII, in-4) we read: – "Noui herbam passim obuiam, quæ si teratur et foueatur manu, donec intepuerit, mox alterius manum detinueris, quoad et illa tebescat amore tui, ille totus continuo ardet, ad aliquot dies. Detinui pedem cuiusdam catuli, hic confestim peregrinum me secutus adeo, quod noctu ante cubiculum ejularet quo eidem aperirem, renunciata hera sua. Adsunt Bruxellæ mihi huius facti testes." (*De Magnetica= vulnerum curatione*, chap. XXVII, p. 708).

This famous plant, whose knowledge is traditional among the Brothers of the Rose + Cross, is none other than *Verbena rustica*. Its use has never been within the reach of black magicians, although its vulgar name can be read –among a thousand others– in all the pages of their Grimoires.

If I speak so without hesitation or ambivalence, it is because first of all –I repeat– the *attractive plant* is designated by its real name in the worst collections of witchcraft. It is above all because its effectiveness depends entirely on the exact astronomical time when it must be picked, and on the essential rites for the preparation of the lightning philtre of which it provides the basis.

By insinuating that it is enough to warm the Verbena in his hand to develop its virtue, Van Helmont gives distorts the conditions required for its authentic use.

He is silent on this point; we must be silent like him.

AVATARS. – This is the name given to the many and varied forms in which a being is incarnated in turn. (See, in Brahmanic theology, the incarnations of Vishnu).

---

3 Birth chart astrology.

B

BAMBOO, BLACK. – A magical plant from the West Indies, used by black sorcerers for their love potions. It can be substituted for *Van Helmont's Attractive Plant* (see this word).

BAPHOMET. – This is the idolatrous figure, or rather the occult symbol, which the Templars were accused of worshipping.

BASILISK. – A fabulous animal on which the most incredible tales have been told. "Just as –says Boguet– that … the mule born of a donkey and a mare: is the Basilisk, born of a cock and a toad." (*Disc. des Sorciers* (Discourse of the sorcerers), Lyon, 1610, in-8, p. 84).
The same demonologer disputes seriously if the Basilisk kills with his gaze, as is notorious for "the Serpent Catoblepas, which makes its home around the Nigris Fountain in Ethiopia, which many believe to be the source of the Nile." (*Ibid.*, p. 187.) Needless to say, Boguet decided in favour of the affirmative.
In our countryside, it is still believed that old cocks lay an egg (!) from which the basilisk comes out.
The Basilisk was one of the familiar faces of the Sabbath… Today there is a small snake of that name, but it seems to be of a different breed, you suffer its look without dying –at least at once– and the natural crown, gemmed with a carbuncle, which made a heraldic crest on the forehead of this singular reptile, has completely disappeared…

BAT. – This nocturnal and silent animal, which is not a bird, but neither looks like a mammal, figures prominently in Satanas' classic menagerie.
Vespertilian blood is used in the composition of a host of spells and charms (see *Evocation*).
Some people consider the Bat to be the protective deity of houses, the *genius loci*, who we must be careful not to destroy or even frighten.
These kind of flying penates[4] are particularly revered in the Caribbean. The unwary person who, at home, would kill one of them, would risk her life.

BEAST OF THE APOCALYPSE. – Fantastic and hieroglyphic animal from the vision of Patmos. Saint John sees it rising from the sea.

BEAU-CIEL-DIEU (GOD). – This is the name of a magical poisoning charge, the composition of which was revealed during the memorable trial of the shepherd Hocque.

---

4 Penates: They were the household gods, who presided over families, and were worshiped in the interior of every dwelling, by the Romans.

BEELZEBUB. – Idol of Syria. The Middle Ages turned Beelzebub into a demon.

BELL. – Bells are commonly attributed with the natural virtue of repelling lightning.

This belief has given rise to a strange practice among devotees. They fight over small silver bells, blessed by the pope, and which Home exports annually by the thousands. When a storm threatens to strike the trees and chop the harvest, the devotees come out with the bell they brandish on the threshold of their farm or house, and –God willing– they ward off lightning and hail, which will fall on the land of the neighbours, ungodly enough not to have procured, in good time, a small silver bell blessed by the Holy Father.

BELPHEGOR. – Another idol of Palestine, which the Christians also made one of the companions of hell.

BEWITCHMENT. – The purpose of this spell is to strike an enemy from a distance. – Sorcerers thus sow death, consumption, disease or any other scourge that Hell has made them dispensers of.

BIRDS. – Some mystical shepherds still derive from the flight of the birds – both lucky and ill-fated–, fateful omens, in the fashion of the ancient augurs.

The universal symbolism of the magicians, which once established connections from one world to another, had attributed bird hieroglyphics to certain cosmogonic powers. Thus the Dove expressed the plastic and configurative virtue of the celestial wife *Ionah*; the Raven, the devouring and compressive force of *Hereb*, the occult agent of the return to essence. The Phoenix was the emblem of substantial homogeneity under the illusory transformations of matter. The Eagle represented the pure Spirit, etc… But soon everything became confused and the tide of general materialisation invaded the science of symbols.

For the Sorcerer, the Eagle is nothing more than a bird whose brain, mixed with food, would cause a certain delirium; the Dove spills its blood in the flask where impure potions are elaborated; the Raven gives a stone that would have the virtue of reconciling enemies, etc… – The Pelican, the Blackbird, the Owl, the Kite, and finally the Hoopoe (already mentioned) are prostituted by the Sorcerer for such ridiculous uses.

BLACK COQ. – The sacrifice of the black rooster is part of the ceremonies of evocation, according to the *Grimoire d'Honorius* (see this word).

In this grimoire we read: "After sunrise, a black rooster shall be killed and the first feather of the left wing shall be taken and kept for use in its time.

The eyes, the tongue and the heart shall be plucked out, dried in the sun, and then ground into powder. At sunset, the rest of the rooster will be buried in a secret place, etc... On Tuesday, at dawn, he (the necromancer) will put the feather of the rooster on the altar, which will be carved with a new penknife, and he will write on clean white paper, with the blood of Jesus Christ (consecrated wine), the figures represented, etc..." (pages 8 and 9 of the alleged edition of Rome, 1760, in-12, with coloured figures).

The theosophist *Amaravella* teaches us that the *sacrifice of the Black Rooster* is part of the rites of trial observed by the *Heung-te* (brothers) of the *San-hohwuy* Chinese society, whose followers are punished by an imperial edict with death. These Heung-té are black magicians, united to do evil (see the *Lotus*, 2nd year, volume IV, n° 22).

BLACK MASS. – An obscene and blasphemous sacrifice, which the Devil and his acolytes celebrated on the Sabbath.

BLOOD. – Blood has a plastic and powerfully expansive virtue, which makes it very suitable for all the operations of the Goetia. But if the magicians of antiquity seem to have spread it in the evocations, only sorcerers nowadays disgrace their rites with these abominable libations.

The spilled blood abundantly engenders the larvae and serves to objectify them.

"Blood is the great sympathetic agent of life; it is the motor of imagination, it is the animated *substratum* of magnetic or astral light, polarised in living beings; it is the first incarnation of the universal fluid; it is materialised vital light. It is made in the image and likeness of infinity; it is a negative substance, in which billions of living and magnetised globules swim and agitate, globules inflated by life and all the vermilion of this elusive fullness... The visions are the delirium of the blood... No one would invent the monsters that his over excitement brings forth; it is the poet of dreams; it is the great hierophant of delirium." – Eliphas Lévi, *La Science des Esprits* (The Science of Spirits).

See, at the word *Carcass*, Porphyry's masterly opinion.

The blood of the doves entered most of the *Philtres*. (See this word.)

BOWL, FATEFUL. – Divination instrument, made of an alloy of the seven mystical metals, with all the letters of the alphabet engraved around the circumference. A ring full of theurgic signs is suspended by a wire above the bowl supported by a tripod – and one evokes the Sibylline geniuses.

This was at least, if we are to believe Ammian, Marcellin and Zosimus, the rite celebrated by some of the courtiers of Emperor Valens, under the direction of the magician Pallade.

The latter pronounced the evocations aloud, standing in the heavy cloud of consecrated perfumes. A laurel wreath girdled his forehead, in the style of the Delphic priests, and a branch of verbena was waving on his right... We saw the ring quivering and swaying at the end of the wire. Suddenly a metallic note tinkled, plaintive; then another, then two more: the ring had struck the Θ of the zodiacal band; then the E, then the O, and finally the Δ. – Théodore! Cried one of the assistants, and it was not considered useful to continue the operation any further that day. (The request made to the Geniuses Rectors of Destiny concerned the successor of Valens Augustus, whose first reply from the Invisibles had prophesied a violent death).

Fatal prediction! Caesar, who had spies everywhere, soon found out everything. His anger was great, made tenfold by his fear. He had Pallade arrested and dragged him to the torture chamber, together with the suspect whom the oracle seemed to have crowned for the scaffold: Theodore. The first syllables of this name sounded to imperial ears like a sacred threat... But where to stop, on the slope of mistrust? Other names also began with the four letters ΘΕΟΔ... and this fateful arrest had struck the tyrant's mind. Anxious that it might be another candidate of Fortune, the Emperor successively condemned to death all *Theodosius, Theodore, Theodat...*

It was a lost cause. The future made it well known that it is possible to evade Caesar's edicts, but not to evade the decrees of Fate. Valens died in a war against the Goths: he was burned at the bottom of a thatched cottage, where he thought he would find an asylum after the defeat – and his successor was in fact Theodosius (the son of one of those whom Valens had killed). The emissaries of death had not been able to discover this young man in Spain, where he was living in seclusion.

Thus the oracle of Pallade was fulfilled, the man with the theurgical bowl.

BOTANOGENY. – Deals with cosmogonical questions related to plants, while botany is the branch of biology that deals with plant life.

BROUCOLAQUES. – Name of the Vampires of Greece; the name alone has changed, the stories are the same.

C

CAMAIEU. – Gaffarel, author of *Curiosités inouïes sur la sculpture talismanique des Persans; Horoscope des Patriarches et lecture des Étoiles* (Unheard-of curiosities on the talismanic sculpture of the Persians; Horoscope of the Patriarchs and reading of the Stars) (Rouen, 1631, in-8, with two planispheres), – Gaffarel names *Gamahez* or *Camaïeux* the stones spontaneously imprinted with certain hieroglyphs, to which he attributes admirable virtues, and which he classifies among the natural talismans.

According to his theory, renewed by Oswald Croll –*Livre des signatures* (Book of Signatures)–, these imprints, often marvellous in their finesse and sharpness, are the signatures of the Elemental Forces that manifest themselves in the three lower kingdoms.

Long before Gaffarel and Crollius, the great Paracelsus knew the Gamaea, whose marvellous virtues he used for his occult medicine. In his works, he dealt with them in great detail and on several occasions, particularly in volume II of his *Opera omnia* (Geneva edition, 1658, 3 vol. in-folio). See, among others, volume II on page 172, column 2e.

CANDLES. – The sorcerers make candles out of tallow of hanging, to garnish the *Hand of Glory* (see this word).

For the black candles of the Sabbath, read Gauffridy's confession. The guests of these assemblies must hold one of these lights in their left hand, when they bend over to kiss the back of Leonardo.

Jérôme Cardan speaks in his works of a *Magic Candle* for the search for treasures. It is also made of human fat; it is adapted to the concave part of a black crescent made of elbow wood, so as to depict the Hebrew Shin (ש), symbol of the elemental fire, or the Sabbath flame between Leonardo's two horns. When, armed with this strange object, one approaches the place where some treasure is buried, the candle begins to spark; this phenomenon is accentuated as one approaches, and the flame goes out when one touches the treasure.

CANTHARIDES. – Flies of a metallic and shiny green colour, which owe to an extremely poisonous alkaloid –Cantharidin– aphrodisiac properties, which sorcerers knew how to take advantage of in the composition of their ointments and their electuaries, to determine the direction of erotic dreams.

CAPUT MORTUUM. – A Latin expression whose literal meaning is "dead head" or "remains", used in alchemy.

CARCASS. – However careful I may be to avoid the dogmatic theories of High Magic for the time being, I cannot bring myself to pass over in silence a page of Porphyry, which is in the first place revealing the profound meaning attributable to the bloody rites of evocation by the sword. Listen to what this theurgist says in substance: "The soul, remaining bound to the body, even after physical death, by a strange tenderness and an affinity all the more narrow as this essence has been separated more abruptly from its envelope, we see souls in great numbers fluttering, all disoriented, around their earthly remains. Moreover, we see them diligently searching for the remains of foreign corpses, and, on all things, for the freshly shed blood, whose vapour seems to restore to them for a few moments certain faculties of life.

"Sorcerers therefore abuse this notion in the exercise of their art. None of them knows how to evoke these souls by force and compel them to appear, either by acting on the remains of the body they have left, or by invoking them in the vapour of the spilled blood." (Porphyry, *Des Sacrifices* (The Sacrifices), chap. II of True Worship).

CAT. – Transformation of women into cats. Berbiguier's antipathy to this animal.

CATOBLEPAS. – It is, according to the demonologist Henry Boguet, a kind of dragon, whose gaze kills, like that of Basilisk (see this word).

Gustave Flaubert gives a completely different description of this fantastic animal: "The Catoblepas, a black buffalo with a pig's head falling to the ground and attached to its shoulders by a thin, long and flabby neck, like an empty gut. He is sprawled completely flat, and his feet disappear under the enormous hard mane that covers his face." (*La tentation de saint Antoine* (The temptation of Saint Anthony), Paris, Lemerre, 1884, small in-12, p. 247).

CHARACTERS. – These are, in Magic, the manifest signs of a verb, or simply expressive signs of an idea. – Isolated, they are called *hierograms*; grouped according to the occult laws into a symbolic whole, they are called *hieroglyphs*. When the hieroglyph appears as a plastic symbol, a painting or a drawing that in itself has an apparent meaning, it becomes an *emblem*. Finally, it is best to call it a *pantacle* if it affects a geometric shape (circular, triangular, stellar, etc.).

The Grimoires are full of strange signs, representative of demons and planetary spirits, and which seem at first glance to be completely indecipherable. This is not the case with most of them. These characters, originally composed according to the rules of an invariable art, have no doubt been altered to the point of becoming unrecognisable at times; no doubt also mystifiers have introduced into these works new signs, scribbled at pleasure, in the absence of any rules, and which it is necessary to know how to recognise and reject at first sight. But for the other characters, it is only a question of finding the key. The Brothers of the Rose + Cross have published this key in a very strange mystical work: *Chymica Vannus* (Amstel., ap. J. Janson., 1666, in-4, fig.). See, for example, pages 55, 62 of the Complement, entitled *Commentatio de pharmaco catholico*; we shall see how the authors,[5] by the

---

5 These authors are called: – "Pro-authoribus Immortalibus Adeptis", seen at the bottom of the title.

methodical combination of radical signs, form hieratic syllables, and compose words by the marriage of these syllables with each other. The adaptation is purely spagyric in *Chymica Vannus*; but this adaptation is only an example proposed; and the rule, remaining identical, can be applied, in a similar way, to the formation of characters in the field of the other sciences which are branches (like the alchemical branch) of the universal strain of Hermes. It is only rarely useful to go very far in the analysis and synthesis of characters. In most cases, the list of zodiacal and planetary signs together constitutes a very passable primitive alphabet, the combinations of which explain and justify the hieroglyphs which seem to be the most rebellious to any interpretation.

In this matter, the *Stéganographie* (Steganography) of Abbot Trithème, especially his *Polygraphie* (Polygraphy), will be fruitfully consulted. Trithème is the great master of secret writings.

See also the *Monas hieroglyphica* of John Dee (in volume II of the *Theatrum chymicum* of Strasbourg, –Argentorati–, 1659).

The characters of the Grimoires are said to be the signatures of certain demons. In order to evoke them, care is taken to trace these characters around the *Magic Circle* (see this word).

CHARM. – A magical preparation.

CHILD'S SKULL. – Sorcerers attribute to the skull of a murdered child the virtue of rendering its bearer invisible. Collin de Plancy, in his *Dictionnaire infernal* (Infernal Dictionary), recounts the trial of a man named Vautrin, sentenced to death by the court of assizes of the Haute-Marne, in February 1857, for having coldly cut the head of a breastfeeding child. He intended to compose a charm of invisibility.

CLAVICLE. – King Solomon is credited with this very strange treatise on the evocation of the Spirits, although no doubt it was written much later, but which was evidently the work of an initiated Rabbi.

It must be said that printed editions of the *Clavicle* are uniformly detestable and uninteresting.

As for the manuscript copies, there are also many notoriously altered and ridiculous ones; but sometimes one finds good copies, studded with a large number of coloured characters and pantacles.

For those who have the key to its hieroglyphics, it is an infinitely precious work; for others, if they believe the text to be deliberately mystifying, they will only be able to get the most false idea of what the Kabbalist master claimed to teach there.

I possess a very beautiful manuscript of the *Clavicle*, translated from Hebrew into French in 1641, and riddled with curious pantacular and talismanic figures. This copy comes from the library of Eliphas Lévi, who took from it the plate he gives (in his *Rituel*), as a revelation of the composition of magnets and the circulatory law of lightning. More complicated in the manuscript, the figure is drawn in red, yellow, blue and black ink and is called the *Great Pantacle*.

CHYLE. – A milky bodily fluid consisting of bile, pancreatic juice and emulsified lipids that is produced in the small intestine of humans and other vertebrates during the digestion of fatty foods, and is taken up by lymphatic vessels specifically known as lactiferous.

COCA OF PERU. – Quite recently introduced in our pharmacopoeias, this vegetable substance is the leaf of the *Erythroxylon coca* (*Malpighiaceae*). The singular property that we know about it, to calm the most stubborn hunger and even to support the body in the absence of any food, made it considered as a tonic and a restorative, moreover rather harmless.

It is certain that Coca, taken in the right dose, acts as a powerful condenser of the vital forces.

On the other hand, this strange product has a sedative property, which it owes to its alkaloid, *Cocaine*: a crumbly, white, bitter and crystalline powder. Cocaine hydrochloride suppresses the most nagging physical pain; the action is sovereign, immediate and absolute: without struggle, the pain gives way and goes away. It is majestic. Neither Chloroform, nor Morphine, nor even Atropine or Hyosciamine offer anything comparable. Awful toothache subsides within a minute. It is to the point where, just by sprinkling Cocaine on the gums, crossed out tooth could be extracted, without the patient even suspecting that the dentist's forceps were there.

It would be expected that innovative practitioners were quick to equip the medical field with such an agent. Coca took its place among the nutritive tonics, stomachic and reconstituting tonics, and its alkaloid was put at the head of the sedatives. Coca wine rivalled that of cinchona itself, and cocaine shots became fashionable.

Unfortunately, the beneficial properties that I have said cannot forbid to classify this plant as one of the most perfidious and dangerous specimens of the plant kingdom.

It is well said that Peruvians, who chew it like betel, can endure twelve hours and more of continuous work in the mines; that they can support the longest and most tiring walks without food, with a load of 100 pounds on their shoulders; but it is not said that Coca takes them to the grave in less than three years. The natives, who have made a habit of this diet, hardly exceed this limit. This is why the Spaniards have made every effort to eradicate in Peru a habit that is so detrimental to their interests, and the Second Council of Lima condemned the use of Coca as early as 1567.

The Peruvians consider the properties of this leaf to be magical, and the wizards of South America make it part of all their evil spells. At the risk of being booed by the positivists, I dare to claim here that Peruvians are not wrong.

Coca, like *hashish* (see this word), but in other ways, exerts a direct and powerful action on the astral body; its customary use loosens in man certain compressive bonds of his hyper-physical nature, bonds whose persistence is a guarantee of salvation for the greatest number.

If I were to speak without hesitation on this point, I would not be believed, even among occultists.

I must confine myself to one piece of advice. – You who value your life, your reason, the health of your soul, avoid hypodermic injections of Cocaine like the plague. Not to mention the habit which is created very quickly (more imperious, more tenacious and more fatal a hundred times than any other of its kind), giving birth to a particular state.

A door has been crossed; a barrier has collapsed. Abruptly introduced into an unknown world, one finds oneself in contact with beings, whose existence was unknown until now.[6] In short, a *tacit pact* has been made.

How did it come about? – By the virtue of blood… This will seem clear, if one has grasped the significance of the few translated lines from Porphyry, about the word *Carcass* (see this word). Blood, as this theosophist suggests, is a magnet for the spiritual powers, for it provides them with the means to objectify themselves and to regain for a moment some of the faculties of life.

It is known that behind all substances, even mineral ones, there are latent virtualities, good or bad, and more or less eager for fleeting objectification. Cocaine is extraordinary in this respect; but I would not advise anyone to bring, even transiently, to the state of nature those beings who escape from the state of essence behind its crystalline veil. The configurative and plastic power of the blood can react on these potential beings and manifest them *outwardly*; but this theurgical mixture has the value of a pact: it will be good to take care of it.

COLOURS. – In practical magic, this is the name given to certain preparations which are applied to the eyes to give the view of spiritual things. – See what

---

6   If one wants to know this world, it is better to enter it through another door than this one.

Nydauld says about them (*De la Lycanthropie* (About Lycanthropy), Paris, 1515, in-8).

In the *Gnome irréconciliable* (Irreconcilable Gnome), a facetious tale in its form, long attributed to the Abbot of Villars, but which is in fact the work of Father Androl, we find a page in which the occult eye drops are discussed. We will transcribe it in its entirety, as it offers amateurs several other details of precious interest: "… I returned to the ceremonial without disgust. I took back the tunic and the mysterious hat; the characters, the fumigations and the lustrations were not forgotten. On my knees, with my face turned to the East, I recited the Enchiridion of Pope Leo; an eye drops made from certain herbs that Psellus used to see the spirits were applied to my eyes; and finally, after I had been made to swallow a few drops of an elixir extracted from an exalted and purified earth, Magnamara sat down on a philosophical chair, and commanded the Prince of the Underground Peoples on behalf of the great God of the Universe, and by virtue of his most holy, august and adorable name, to go to his chamber at that very hour. He obeyed the voice of the philosopher and introduced himself. Magnamara then raised his eye-drops, and I saw the Prince of the Gnomes clearly before me." (*Le comte de Gabalis, ou Entretiens sur les sciences secrète* (The Count of Gabalis, or Interviews on the Secret Sciences), new edition, London, Vaillant, 1742, 2 vols. in-12. – Volume II, pp. 141-142).

COMETS. – Comets have always been considered as harbingers of the most lamentable tribulations: wars, devastation, plagues, famine, calamities of all kinds.

CROSS. – Boguet had a woman named Françoise Secretan burned as a witch because the cross of her rosary was chipped. This, it seems, was an extremely serious and revealing clue for the judge (see *Discours des sorciers* (Discourse of the Sorcerers), p. 295).

D

DECANTER. – A forecasting tool, from which Cagliostro in particular has benefited greatly. Either a decanter full of crystal-clear water, or a magnetised crystal ball; it was in such environments, very refractive for astral light, that he made his *Doves'* eyes float for a long time. He named young boys who were still innocent, or girls who played the role of *passive seers*, while he held them under the irradiation of his magnetic will. These little beings then saw the chain of future contingents unfold in the form of a series of images that were obviously sibylline, a sort of concrete prophecy, which was only waiting to be translated into demotic language. The Doves expressed themselves with exclamations. Suddenly Cagliostro, with an inspired and vibrant voice, improvised an oratory or dithyrambic commentary, and the most mocking souls and the most sceptical minds were then subjugated.

It is said that in the early years of her marriage, Marie-Antoinette of Austria, still being Madame la Dauphine, wanted to consult the oracle, persisting in her whim, despite all the objections of the Magician, who finally complied only to obey a formal order. – What dreadful mirage did the Dauphine see condensed in the dazzling crystal? – She never says; but it seems certain that the spectacle was terrible, for she fainted in that place.

This is only a legend, perhaps greatly embellished by passing from mouth to mouth. In any case, after 93, her memories were brought together, and once upon a time she was enlightened. It was said that Cagliostro showed the daughter of the Caesars a scaffold erected in the midst of a tumultuous rabble; an executioner whose hand, already stained with august blood, struck a queen at the foot of a log; then a metal triangle falling like lightning, and a head –that of the unfortunate spectator herself– a blond and charming head rolling in the basket of her!

DEMON, BEARDED. – The alchemists of the Rose+Croix school attribute the success of the Philosopher's Stone to the intervention of a *bearded demon*. This demon, a symbolic representation of the *Anima mundi*, is none other than the *Baphomet* of the Templars (see this word). It is the living 🜍, born from the fecundation ☿ of the philosopher's with the golden ♀.

DEMONS. – Jean Wier, in his treatise *de Lamiis*, gives a very complete and detailed list of the infernal hierarchies, under this title: *Pseudo-monarchia Dæmonum*. – Princes and great dignitaries, Ministers, Ambassadors, Justiciers, Officers of the House of Lucifer, Master of Ceremonies, nothing is missing, – even the steward of small pleasures!

The good Wier certainly wanted to use the ridiculous as a terrible weapon against the champions of Anthropomorphic Demonology.

DIVINATION (instruments of). – They are innumerable; the *Tarot* must be placed at the head (see this word).

Let us also mention birds, egg whites, coffee grounds, clear water, fire, earth, and a thousand other objects that diviners flatter themselves to ask questions about. In the words *Decanter and Bowl, fateful*, we will find details on two very curious kinds of divination.

For the rest, I refer to Gaspar Peucer, whose work, translated into French by Simon Goulard de Senlis, is the most complete work of its kind: *Des Devins, ou commentaires des principales sortes de divination* (Diviners, or commentaries on the main kinds of divination), divided into XV books, in which Satan's tricks and impostures are discovered, etc… (in Antwerp, by Hevdrick Connix, 1587, 1 vol., very large in-8, of 700 pages).

DIVINING ROD. – It is a forked branch of beech, alder or hazel, stripped of its bark; one of the branches of the forked end is held in each hand, and the divining rod inclines itself towards the ground, to indicate the underground presence of a spring, a treasure, or the hiding place of a criminal.

Physique occulte (Occult physics), by the Abbot of Vallemont (La Haye, Moëtjens, 1690, 2 vol. small in-8, frontisp. and peculiar engravings), is entirely devoted to the study of the divining rod. It gives a theory of physics, the refutation of which R.P. Lebrun endeavoured at length in his *Histoire critique des Pratiques superstitieuses* (Critical History of Superstitious Practices) (Amsterdam, 1737, 3 vol. in-8, fig.). Two out of three large volumes are devoted to it.

DOVE. – This charming bird, once dedicated to Venus, plays a great role in the making of the *Philtres* (see this word)..

DRUM, MAGIC. – It is used by Siberian Tatars to make the Devil appear. It is a type of Basque drum, scribbled with hieroglyphic signs; it is called *Kamlat*. A deafening cacophony prefigures the evocations; the sorcerer capering, gesticulating and shouting accompanies his sound instrument. Finally, the Devil appears in the form of a monstrous bear, running from parts of the North: but it is most often to beat the evocator.

E

EGG (White of). – Configurative and refractive material for astral light. Many modern sibyls successfully practice divination by egg white.

ELVES. – Demons or genies, spirits of light or darkness, in the mythology of the Edda. Demonologists want to see devils.

ENCHANTED ROD. – This rod, also called lightning rod, gives power over the infernal hierarchies. At least that is what the grimoires ensure.

To prepare this rod, a forked stick of wild hazelnut is shod at both ends, with the iron of a cutlass that was used to gorge a *kid* (a small child). Care is taken to magnetise these two frameworks, to reserve the skin of the victim, which is cut into a single circular strip; and to draw the *Circle* (see this word), this strip is fixed to the ground with nails torn from the coffin of a child who died without baptism, etc.

ENCHIRIDION. – One can say of the *Enchiridion* what I have already said of the *Clavicles of Solomon*. All the printed editions are deliberately altered, as are most of the manuscripts bearing this title. However, it is not impossible, with perseverance, to discover a good manuscript copy of this collection, rich in mysterious formulas, and above all in pantacular figures, where the entire interest lies, for the bibliophile as well as for the occultist. It is claimed that Pope Leo III, who received from Charlemagne the territory on which the popes' subsequent claim to temporal power was based, thought he was paying homage to the monarch with usury in this cabalistic book.

One of the least bad Latin editions is that of Rome, 1670, in-12: *Enchiridion Leonis Popæ, serenissimo imperotori Carolo Magno in munus pretiosum datum, nuperrimè mendis omnibus purgatum.*

The French editions, especially the so-called Rome edition, by Fr. Angelo de Rimini, S. D. (c. 1850), vol. in-12, fig., are unspeakable speculations from the low bookshops.

EPHIALTES. – Smothering incubus for the Greeks; *Insultor* of the Latins. See the words *Incubus, Succubus.*

EVOCATION (Instruments necessary for). – In the *Rituel* of Eliphas Lévi we read: "One must choose a solitary and deprecated place, such as a cemetery haunted by evil spirits, a dreaded ruin in the countryside, the cellar of an abandoned convent, the place where an assassination was committed, a druidic altar or an ancient temple of idols.

"One must be equipped with a seamless, sleeveless black robe; a lead cap studded with the signs of the Moon, Venus and Saturn; two candles of human tallow, planted in black wooden crescent-shaped candlesticks; two crowns of verbena; a magic sword with black handle; a magic fork; a copper vase containing the victim's blood; a incense holder containing the perfumes, which will be camphor, aloe, ambergris, storax, incorporated and kneaded with goat, mole and bat blood; four nails, torn from the coffin of a victim; the head of a black cat, fed with human flesh for five days; a bat drowned in its blood; the horns of a goat *cum quo puella concubueritit*, and the skull of a parricide.

"All these horrible and rather difficult to gather together objects, are put together for the evocation."

F

FARFADETS.[7] – Familiar, mischievous and good-natured elves, to whom the legend attributes a rather beneficial influence. But Berbiguier, diverting this

---

7 Farfadets are creatures of French folklore. The word translates variously as "Sprite", "Imp", "Brownie", or "Leprechaun", though they also resemble the Pixies of Britain's West Country.

term from its traditional meaning, immortalised it by applying it to demons and especially to the invisible sorcerers who persecute them.

But I have promised to say a word about the weapons he uses to put these rascals on the run. One could write a long chapter on the magical arsenal of Berbiguier alone. His means of defence are very similar to the means of attack used by those under the jurisdiction of Lancre and Boguet.

He exterminates or captures the Goblins, his persecutors. (Facsimile of an engraving from the book *Des Farfadets*).

"Jesus Christ was sent to earth to wash mankind of its sins. I am perhaps destined to destroy the enemies of the Most High."

This is the clear and laconic epigraph of the book of the *Farfadets*. – Let us see how the new Messiah proceeds to destroy these monsters vomited by Hell. I will summarise his compelling explanations:

The first thing to obtain is an ox heart, which will be boiled in a pot, with two pints of water. When the heat has sufficiently softened it, pins, nails and wooden splinters will be put in it, exclaiming in a terrible voice: "Let everything I do serve as payment: I am sorry for the worker of Beelzebub".

Then this viscera will be nailed to a table with three stab wounds, repeating the imprecations;

Salt and sulphur will be thrown into the fire which boils the pot;

When you feel the Farfadets, in various forms of invisible animals, entering at night into the mystery of the alcoves and walking, jumping, getting familiar with even the most intimate attitudes, in a deplorable tête-à-tête, you will prick them sharply on the sheets with a punch or bacon;

Or else tobacco may be thrown in their faces, and while they are rolling blind and dizzy, they will be collected pell-mell with the tobacco powder, and enclosed in hermetically sealed jars, where a few pinches of fresh tobacco and cayenne pepper, with a little good vinegar, will be added from time to time. – What a salad! "Tobacco is their food and vinegar quenches their thirst. So they live in a state of discomfort, and they will witness my daily triumphs; I place my bottles so that they can see every day what I do against their comrades…" (See *Les Farfadets*, Volume III, p. 227).

"Another way of waging war on the Farfadets is to kill all the toads that can be caught in the countryside: toads are acolytes of the spirits of hell." (Volume III, p. 229.)

We know Berbiguier's defensive weapons.

Let us conclude by examining his telescope: "*My revealing bucket* is a wooden vase, which I fill with water; it serves to reveal the Farfadets when they are in the clouds…" (Tome III, p. 229). This bucket… placed on my window, repeats to me in the water all the operations of my enemies: I see them crossing, arguing, jumping, dancing and flying, much better than all the *Forioso* and *Saqui* of the earth. I see them when they ward off the weather, when they pile up clouds, when they lighten lightning and thunder. The water that is in the bucket follows all the movements of these wretches (*sic*). I see them, sometimes in the form of a snake or an eel, sometimes in the form of a monkey or a hummingbird... – Unbelievers, look at my bucket, and you will no longer upset me with your denials!" (Pages 225-226 of Volume III.)

Berbiguier describes all these fine operations in a seductive phrase: *my works.*

It is thought that the bad jokers, seeing the good man in these dispositions of mind, would take pleasure in having him skimmed from the Inferno of the apocalyptic letters, which he has conscientiously collated among the supporting documents.

Let us conclude with some of these extracts: – "*The ambassador of the Evil Spirits, Rothomago, on the fifth day of the moon, to M. Berbiguier, exterminator of the infernal cohort.*

"Berbiguier, will you stop tormenting me and all my colleagues? Miserable that you are! You have just killed fourteen hundred of my subjects, and I was almost a victim on the day of your work, when I was in the pipe of your stove! If you would be more lenient with us, we would call you our sovereign.... You would be the head of all minds; you would enjoy not only this great advantage, but also the advantage of possessing all the beautiful women who would be in your palace; for you must know that we have here all the queens, the princesses, and finally all the most beautiful women who, for 4800 years, have made the delights of all the greatest heroes of this world! ... See and consent, and you will be the happiest of all mortals; otherwise... we will come en masse to fight you with torches, to exterminate you in the course of the summer...

The extraordinary ambassador: ROTHOMAGO."

(Volume III, p. 417, *passim*.)

Other epistle:

"Of the infernal and invisible Committee...

Farfaderico-parafarapines! Tremble, Berbiguier... It is we, Moreau, the Vandeval, who write to you; we, whom you lacerated yesterday with seven mortice pins, we whom you denounced to the priest.... You also enjoy, from time to time, revealing the sacred mysteries of the *Opoteosoniconiga-menaeo* to the first to come. – Tremble with fear!... Nothing will protect you against our revenge, neither your fat Levite of a robe, nor your left side pocket where you put your coins, which will always be full of our claws, nor

your voluptuous puddings that serve as a throne for love, and from which the line that wounded the heart of our tender Feliciadoïsca started. What had she done to you, wretch!... An old Rodrigue[8] like you, whom a sixteen-year-old girl wanted to take with her, is there anything to cry for help?..."
(I stop in time; it becomes indecent...)
"If you want to enter our society, all you have to do is say yes aloud on the 16th of February at 3.13 p.m.; then you will be well received; you will be taken away in a zephyrean gondola, which will take you to a place of delights where you will enjoy *ad libitum*.
"Farewell. – Signed: Moreau and Vandeval." (T. III, pp. 309-310, *passim*.)
Poor Berbiguier!...

FLUIDIC FORM. – It is the astral body, the ethereal double of the physical body, capable of projecting itself outwards and acting at a distance, while the body rests motionless.

FLYING PISTOL. – It is a diabolical coin, endowed with a singular virtue: faithful to its first owner, it returns of its own accord to its original owner, to the great detriment of the unfortunate innkeeper to whom it was given as payment. The next day, the innkeeper only finds a dry leaf, of alder or birch, in the place where he put the coin.

FUMIGATIONS. – It is the fragrant smoke of the consecrated perfumes, which are burnt in ceremonial magic operations, and by name in the theurgical evocations (see the word *Perfumes*).

G

GHOULS. – The Ghouls are the witches who devour unspeakable carrion on the Sabbath, and who dig up the dead in the cemeteries to feed on their shreds. The Salic law condemns them under the name of *striges*; it fines them.

GNOMES. – Elemental spirits. – See Paracelsus and the *Comte de Gabalis* (Count of Gabalis), by the Abbot of Villars. The Gnomes haunt the underground chasms.

GRIMOIRES. – As a general rule, this is the name given to all the books of superstitious magic, all the collections of abominable recipes, interspersed with blasphemous formulas. In the past, the Grimoires were carefully searched for in order to destroy them, and often the unfortunate ones found with these kinds of manuals were punished with death.

---

8 Rodrigue is a character from Corneille's play *le Cid*, a dashing hero torn between passion for Chimène and duty towards his family and country.

Le grand Grimoire, avec la grande Clavicule de Salomon, la Magie noire et les forces infernales du grand Agrippa (The Great Grimoire, with the Great Clavicle of Solomon, the Black Magic and the infernal forces of the great Agrippa), etc. S.L.N.D. in-18, is undoubtedly one of the most curious; but no one is as famous as *Le Grimoire du pape Honorius, avec un recueil des plus rares secrets* (The Grimoire of Pope Honorius, with a collection of the rarest secrets), Rome, 1670, in-16. Coloured circles and figures. (Now almost impossible to find.) – "This Grimoire is not unimportant to the curious of science. At first glance, it seems to be nothing more than a web of revolting absurdities; but for those initiated into the signs and secrets of the Kabbalah, it becomes a veritable monument to human perversity; the Devil is shown as an instrument of power... The doctrine of this Grimoire is the same as that of Simon and most Gnostics; the passive principle substitutes the active principle, passion, therefore, is preferred to reason; deified sensualism; woman put before man, a tendency that is found in all anti-Christian mystical systems; this doctrine is expressed by a pantacle placed at the head of the book. The moon of Isis occupies the centre; around the selenic crescent are three triangles which form a single triangle; the triangle is surmounted by a double-crossed ansate cross; around the triangle which is inscribed within a circle, and in the interval formed by the three segments of the circle, on one side is the sign of the spirit and the Kabbalistic seal of Solomon; on the other, the magic knife and the initial letter of the Binary; below, an upside down cross, forming the figure of the lingam, and the name of God אל also upside down; around the circle, one reads these words traced in the form of a legend: *Obey your superiors and be submissive to them, because they are careful to do so.*" (*Historie de la Magie* (History of Magic), by Eliphas Lévi).

These lines of Abbé Constant say more than I can add. This excellent magician was very busy in his works of the Grimoire d'Honorius; one must read –*Clef des grands Mystères* (Key to the Great Mysteries)– the magnificent and sinister story of the priest Verger, preluding, by infernal evocations and assiduous reading of the Grimoire, to the furious mania which was to make him a murderer.

I have already transcribed a page from the *Grimoire d'Honorius*, about the *Black Cock* (see this word).

The copy in my possession –allegedly an edition of Rome, 1760, in-12; in reality a modern reprint from Lille, Blocquel ed.– bears on its last page four diabolical signatures (enclosed), bloody characters which have been traced neither with a pen nor perhaps with a brush:

These are the most notoriously satanic and blasphemous hieroglyphics I have ever seen in my life:

A stick with three forked crosspieces, with two square dots at the base;

A black triangle, between two baphometic horns;

An inverted Shin (ש);

An opaque hand, the five fingers extended, under the inverted ש; this hand symbolizes the negation of the pentagrammatic dogma.

I had the colouring matter (reddish-brown) that was used to trace them analysed: it is blood.

The paper is yellowed all around, or rather scorched like a candle flame.

Without going any further into my inductions, I conclude that this Grimoire was the property of a witchcraft adept.

Among the most singular and rare Grimoires, one must also mention the work entitled *La Sexte-Essence dialectique et potentielle, tirée d'une nouvelle façon d'alambiquer, suivant les préceptes de la sainte Magie et l'Invocation des Démons* (The Dialectic and potential Sixth-Essence, drawn from a new way of convolution, following the precepts of Holy Magic and the Invocation of the Demons (Paris, 1595, in-8.) – Highly peculiar; particularly recommended to lovers of ambiguous mysticism.

H

HASHISH. – This is the name given by Orientals to the fatty extract of Indian hemp (*Cannabis indica*), prepared with the flowering tops, which is reduced to the consistency of an ointment by a special process.

The same hemp, smoked like tobacco, is called *Kief*.

The smoke of the kief, and especially the assimilation of hashish (taken pure in the form of a bowl, or mixed with a date preserve), gives a particular, otherworldly intoxication, which is prized by certain natures, mystical and sensual all together, as a foretaste of the heavenly happiness of the chosen ones.

One must read Baudelaire's *Paradis artificiels* (Artificial paradises), where the poet's style surpasses, in precise erudition and didactic firmness, the usual language of scholars. It is marvellous to see with what wisdom Baudelaire decomposes the psychic action of this strange ingredient, which has the power to exalt joy or exacerbate pain,[9] bringing to the superlative the feeling that dominated the soul the minute it was ingested. It is an expansive director of passions and latent ideas; through it, the Unconscious manifests itself to the amazed Consciousness – and the soul, contemplating itself in its own mirror, reveals itself positively to itself.

In this way, we meet a friend from within, whom we never suspected; we talk with our guardian angel, or, if we prefer, with the instigator of perdition that each of us carries within.

Before the fall of Eden, the universal man had the almost divine faculty to objectify all his ideas. If he thought of beings, he created them by dreaming. Now it seems that hashish restores for an hour to the individual man that ineffable power to effortlessly exteriorise everything whose image he carries within him. It seems that the creative verb is returned to him, as he possessed it before his sin.

Thus, by the virtue of hashish, man evades or seems to evade the sentence that was pronounced against him, in the person of Eve, his volitional faculty: *I will multiply your labours and your conceptions. In pain shall you give birth...* and that the agnostic Bibles render with these words: *I will multiply the evils and the groans of your pregnancies; you will give birth in pain.*

Indian hemp is a magical herb, in the first place.

HIGH-HUNT. – In some parts of Lorraine and the northern provinces of France, the air transportation of sorcerers on the Sabbath is known as the "High Hunt".

HIPPOMANES. – Singular growth which, according to some authors, grows on the head of foals. This fleshy substance, used in a large number of philtres and charms, is said to be highly endowed with aphrodisiac virtues. This is, in any case, what demonographers are unanimous in claiming.

HOOPOE. – Common bird especially in Asia Minor: it is said that one sometimes finds in its nest a miraculous stone whose possession confers supernatural powers. – It is this stone which must be set as the stone of a ring, to make it a ring of invisibility.

---

9 The exaggeration of painful feelings only manifests itself in experiences made unexpectedly, blindly and without preparation; for hashish, taken in full knowledge of the facts, on the contrary heals the wounds of an ulcerated soul. It is enough to concentrate one's will on the senses; for the exercise of will, abolished or at least blunted in the region of physical activity, becomes all-powerful in the internal and virtual sphere. Nevertheless –to take an example– there can be no doubt that among the pusillanimous, hashish extends terror to the borders of delirium. The temptation to commit suicide is frequent; one is asked to flee, in death itself, the fear of death.

HUMOUR, HUMOURS. – Early modern physicians, basing their understanding of the body mainly on the Hippocratic texts of the 4th century BC, gave an overarching and primary role to four bodily fluids called humours (blood, phlegm, melancholy and choler). These humours corresponded to even more basic aspects of nature: the four Aristotelian elements (air, water, earth and fire), the four combinations of primary qualities (hot and humid, cold and humid, cold and dry, hot and dry), the four seasons of the year, the four temperaments (sanguine, phlegmatic, melancholic and choleric), and so on. Since Hippocrates, the humoral theory was the most common view of the functioning of the human body among European physicians until the advent of modern medicine in the mid-19th century.

I

IDOL. – Material representation of a Divinity, taken by the vulgar profane for that very Divinity. Idols can be considered as incarnations of Satan.

ILLUMINATI. – It is treated at length in our *Seuil du Mystère* (Mystery Threshold) –*De deux sociétés secrètes* (Of two secret societies) en 1890 and *Discours d'initiation Martiniste* (Martinist Initiation Discourse) in 1890.

IMMORTALITY (Elixir of). – The alchemists were said to have composed, with the philosopher's stone, a universal medicine or Elixir of Life, which, according to some, prolonged existence beyond normal limits, and according to others, ensured immortality to all those who agreed to regulate its use. Read *Zanoni*, the superb magic novel by Sir E. Bulwer Lytton. See also the very curious revelations published in the *Lotus*, 1ˢᵗ year, N° 2 and 3, under this title: *L'Élixir de Vie*, under the signature: a *Chela*. – Who is not familiar with the traditional and symbolic legends of the Fountain of Youth and the water of eternal youth? Cagliostro and St. Germain were said to have the secret.

INCUBUS. – Unclean ghosts of the male sex who rape women in their sleep; as opposed to Succubi (see this word), female ghosts who abuse men and disappoint their dreams. By extension, Incubi and Succubus have been named *Incubus* and *Succubus*, all invisible, supposed to have a love trade with mortals (see *Ephialtes*).

INFIDELITY. – The use of ordeal potions (unnamed mixtures, frequently used in the Middle Ages and served to the suspected wife in the *Chalice of Suspicion*) dates back to the best times of Israel.
The wife who persisted in claiming to be innocent was subjected, by order of the Great Consistory, to the trial of the *Waters of Bitterness*. A priest care-

fully collected dust from the tabernacle, mixing a pinch of it with the juice of bitter herbs in a little water. This was the drink that the unhappy person had to swallow in one gulp, at the very door of the Holy of Holies.

If guilty, she died, says the Legend, her eyes rolling and in horrible convulsions; if the drink had no effect on her, the young woman was honourably dismissed: her innocence could no longer be disputed.

K

KALI. – Goddess of murder, among the Hindus. Her followers constitute the formidable secret society of the *Stranglers* or *Thugs*.

L

LACES. – They were used for ligatures of all kinds, especially for the *Aiguillette* knot (see this word).

LAMPS. – A thousand tales have been told about the marvellous and perpetual lamps. One of them is said to have thrown a strange light in the sepulchre of Tullia, daughter of Cicero, after so many centuries.

Gosset published a very curious dissertation on sepulchral lamps, following his work entitled: *Révélation cabalistique sur la Médecine universelle* (Kabbalistic Revelation on Universal Medicine), 1735, 1 vol. petit in-8.

LARVAE. – Inconsistent fantastic substances, but real, devoid of their own essence and living a borrowed life. They attach themselves to those who gave birth to them and who, in the long run, exhaust themselves in feeding them.

LEMURES. – Larvae with perverse instincts. It was thought that they could be the damned souls, who have returned to this world to help the demons in their infernal task of proselytism.

LEONARD. – This is the demon who presides over the Sabbaths, most often in the form of a monstrous goat.

LEVIATHAN. – The Talmudists give this name to the androgynous Spirit of Evil. Considered in its male incarnation, it is Sammael, (see this word) or the *Insinuating Serpent*, and in its female incarnation it is *Lilith* (see this word).

LILITH, – or the *Tortuous Snake*. Lilith is the wife of Sammael (see this word) and the female incarnation of Leviathan (see this word).

M

MAGIC CAKE. – Cakes baked on the kidneys of the Queen of the Sabbath were distributed at the Black Mass. The *Confarreatio* is the devil's communion.

MAGIC CIRCLE. – It is a circumference traced on the ground and in the centre of which one stands, in ceremonial magic experiences, especially when evoking spirits; a protective barrier that cannot be crossed without falling into the power of the fantastic beings who have been able to respond to the evocation. As long as one remains sheltered by this mysterious rampart (symbol of the collective will, good or bad, with which one is in communion), one runs no risk.

At least that is what the sorcerers ensure. They add that if one strikes with a magic *wand* (see this word), one of the demons that crowd around the circle, under the appearance of screaming monsters, he is immediately forced to enter the circle and obey the wizard; he can only regain his freedom after having been discharged.

As for these circles of thick and dark greenery, which one finds in the meadows, and which stand out in force against the uniform colour of the surrounding grass, the peasants call them *Fairy Circles*.

MAGIC MIRROR. – The story goes like this: the Sagas of Thessaly used to trace their cryptic formulas in blood on these mirrors: the moon –another mirror– would immediately reflect these bloody characters and the answer would then be printed on its silver crescent. This is how the Oracle was rendered.

Later, mirrors were made from the seven metals of Hermes. The most common mirrors are made of pewter, studded with devilish signs or pantacles. These objects only had the name of the mirror. They were not polished, but in the long run, when you looked at them, your imagination became excited; a halo blurred the contours of the enlarged disc, and prophetic images were confusedly drawn on it.

The Baron du Potet's mirror consists of a circle sprinkled with small coals – a favourable medium for the refraction of images.

All these mirrors impress the sensitive by virtue of the same law. Cagliostro's *decanter* (see this word) is itself, all in all, a magical mirror of another form.

In the ceremonial operations of Theurgy, concave mirrors are placed on the four walls of the occult cabinet.

MAGIC PLANTS. – The attractive plant is not the only one endowed with occult properties of marvellous energy. The ancient magicians knew XXII plants, whose virtue corresponded to the esoteric meaning of the XXII arcana of the Absolute Doctrine. Verbena referred to Arcanum VI (the lover of the Tarot).

The magicians of the Middle Ages had only been able to collect the wrecks of these traditions. Late heirs of a science that had fallen, though still real,[10] they reduced the list of sacred plants to sixteen names. Again the numerical order of the normal classification was inverted, and unfortunate substitutions further altered an already unrecognisable nomenclature.

According to César Longin, the sixteen sacred plants are:

Heliotrope (*Ireos* of the Chaldeans), the herb of sincerity;
Nettle (*Roybra*), the herb of bravery;
Virga pastoris (*Lorumborat*), the grass of fertility;
Celidoine (*Aquilaris*), the grass of triumph;
Periwinkle (*Iterisi*), the grass of fidelity;
Catnip (*Bieith*), the herb of vitality.
Dog's Tongue (*Algeil*), the grass of sympathy;
Henbane (*Mansesa*), the herb of death;
Lily (*Augo*), the grass of manifestation;
Mistletoe (*Luperax*), the herb of salvation;
Centaury (*Isiphilon*), the herb of enchantment;
Sage (*Coloricon*), the herb of life;
Verbena (*Ophanas*), the herb of love;
Lemon balm (*Celeivos*), the grass of comfort;
Rose (*Eglerisa*), the initiatory herb;
Serpentine (*Cartulin*), the herb of fluids.

MAGIC WORDS. – The sorcerer prefers them incomprehensible, because his Creed is none other than that of Tertullian: *quia absurdum*. – On the reason and virtue of barbaric words and unintelligible names.

MAGICAL POISONING CHARGE. – This is the name given to the charms composed to kill cattle; they are buried at the threshold of stables or sheepfolds. – See Hocque's trial (p. 97-98).

MAGNET. – Once thought to be a magical poison, sorcerers used to pound it and make it part of their charms (see this word).

The *wand* of the Magician (see this word) was hollow and contained a magnetic steel rod.

According to Marcellus Empiricus, the magnet cured headaches.

The Basilide sectarians used it as a talisman (see this word) against the power of evil spirits.

MAGNETISM. – It is the art of physiologically influencing a person (who takes the name of subject), of substituting the subject's own will; in a word, the

---

10 The Science of the Neo Magi of Chaldea.

art of sovereignly taking over his organs, so as to make him do what he does not want to do and to prevent him from doing what he wants. This habitual fact of the intrusion of a foreign will, which replaces the will of the subject, should be called subjection. The isolated phenomenon of transmission to the subject of a particular will, to which he will obey, is called suggestion.

Hypnotic sleep is one of the most banal manifestations of magnetism; while the subject sleeps, he is, so to speak, like soft wax between the fingers of the magnetiser. But it is a mistake to believe that suggestion can only be practised during sleep, and in many cases it works wonderfully on perfectly awake subjects.

Magnetism, conceived in its broadest sense, embraces a very large part of the phenomena which can be realised; its domain extends far and wide, in the sphere of practical magic.

MALEFICES. – In general, any spell or superstitious operation, with the aim of harming one's neighbour.

MANDRAKE. – The Mandrake (*Atrope Mandrogora*) is a narcotic and poisonous plant, of the *Solanaceae* family, very close cousin of the Belladonna (*Atropa Belladona*).

It is well known that all the toxic Solanaceae, such as Morella, Belladonna, Datura, etc., were used in the same way as Hemlock, Oenanthus and Hemp in the preparation of magic ointments. But the Mandrake offers other titles to our curiosity. Its root, bristling with tufted filaments, most often affects the figure of the thighs or genitals;[11] it also sometimes displays the outline of a human head.

According to an old tradition, man first appeared on earth in the form of monstrous mandrakes, animated by an instinctive life, and that the breath from above ever-greened, transmuted, disintegrated, and finally uprooted, to become beings endowed with their own thought and movement.

Also, in the Middle Ages, it was the dream or the delirium of certain followers, aspiring to the *Vital Mastery*, to find the composition of the original-principle, in order to make mandrakes grow; to react and be aroused to the mental life, by the infusion of the *Archon*.

Others, less ambitious, were content to obtain false *Teraphim* (see this word), by evoking a *larvae* (see this word), in a mandrake cut in human form; a hideous idol that they conjured up to make oracles… It is hard to imagine the furious madness to which superstition led them! It was from under the gallows that they went to fetch the mandrake; to pull it out of the

---

11 Which has made it appear to be an aphrodisiac, according to the theory of natural *signatures*, already touched upon in the word *Camaieu*.

ground, they tied a dog's tail to its root and hit it with a mortal blow. The poor beast in agony, struggling, uprooted the mandrake. Then (they believed) the sensitive soul of the dog would pass through the mandrake and, out of sympathy, attract the spiritual soul of the hanged man…

Other sorcerers forged a metallic *Android*, hoping to confer on him the gift of speech.

By extension, Mandrakes, *Androids*, *Homunculus* and *Teraphim* were called Mandrakes; they even came to name any magical preparation capable of rendering an oracle in this way.

See the words: *Android* and *Teraphim*.

MARKS. – Stigmata imprinted by the Devil on the bodies of his acolytes.

Leonard has his *controllers*, who stamped wizards and witches, just as metals are stamped at the Mint. The mark most often affects the features of a toad, a hare, a mouse, etc… The place is insensitive to stings, and pinpricks do not make even a drop of blood spurt out. The mark is sometimes on the forehead or in the eye, more usually at the folds of the mucous membranes and in the most secret parts of the body.

The surgeons are therefore charged with visiting the accused, and with planting needles in all places of the body where it is supposed that the Devil's signature can be concealed. And woe to the poor accused who neglects to cry out every time the sharp point touches his flesh. He is lost in advance. Often, like Lancre in the land of Labourt, the judge charges the repentant witch (who saved her skin by a spontaneous confession) with this long, barbaric and meticulous search, on the person of all the accomplices denounced by her. I would suggest that the unfortunate witch is displaying an abominable zeal, in order to buy, as far as she is concerned, the clemency of the magistrate.

Pierre de Lancre was gallant by nature; so all the witches who knew they were passable had only one dream, to dodge the scaffold and escape through the alcove, stepping over the judge's bed.

Lancre's favourite was a fifteen-year-old girl called the Murgui, a fierce denunciator of her former friends, who, having been sent by the judge to find the *stigma Diaboli* on them, preferred to martyr the prettiest – her possible rivals of the next day!

This is what Michelet (*La Sorcière* (The Sorceress), p. 221) and M. Jules Baissac (*Les grands jours de la sorcellerie* (Great days of witchcraft), p. 401) suggest; it is what seems to emerge from Lancre's own narrative.

MELICERTES. – The *King of the Earth* (root: טואדלמ); bloody deity, whose idol was raised in Tenedo.

MENDES (goat of). – Raised in the temple of God, his mission was to sacrifice the modesty of the young Egyptian girls.

MOCHLATH. – One of the four wives of *Sammael* (see this word), in the Caco-pneumatics of the Kabbalists.

MOLE. – The blood of the mole was used in a great number of philtres and electrical goods.

MOLOCH. – The devouring idol of Moloch stood wherever the Phoenicians had settlements and colonies.

MONSTERS. – They were said to be born of the Devil's impure trade with Witches.

Miserable followers of Goetia sometimes obtained nameless monsters, by throwing, according to the energetic word of Eliphas Lévi, human seed into animal soil. A small number of these monsters come to term, but almost all of them expire a few days after birth. As for the very few that become adults, they have no chance of coming of age – being blasphemous blasphemies of Nature, which lies to itself, always with regret.

N

NAGUAL. – Mexican Nagualism is not without analogy with European Lycanthropy. It is a pact of tacit solidarity, of offensive and defensive alliance, between a man and an animal: the sanction of such a pact is in the reality of the occult bond that unites them.

The Nagual is a crocodile, a lion, a snake, a bird, or any other animal, to which the native has been attached, since childhood, by an indissoluble fluidic bond. The ceremony that consecrates this bond is very similar to an initiation…

Therefore, for each *initiated* native, the Nagual is an *alter ego*; and all his life, man remains coupled to this beast that cherishes and protects him, sharing his adventurous existence, his good and bad luck, his sorrows and joys, suffering from the evil from which he himself suffers. This strange solidarity cannot be doubted; the facts of Nagualism are certified by the most honourable and least suspicious testimonies.

Example of Nagualism, guaranteed by the R. P. Burgoa:

A huge crocodile attacks the R.P. Diégo, as it was riding a horse on the shore of a lake. Skilful and vigorous enough to break free at once, this priest spurs his horse, and, brandishing his shod stick, charges the monster, which is still trying to drag him to the bottom of the lake. The mount's kicks are no small help to the missionary, during this duel of a new kind. In short, he can go his own way, leaving the crocodile for dead on the shore.

But back at the Mission's headquarters, the first news Father Diego is told is the inexplicable agony of a young Indian boy, whom he had punished a few days before, with extreme rigour… Once checked, the Indian was wearing all the wounds made to his *Nagual*. This young man died – and at the same time the crocodile was breathing out at the water's edge. (Detailed details of the adventure can be read in chapter LXXI of the *Description géographique de la province de Santo-Domingo* (Geographical Description of the Province of Santo Domingo), by R. P. Burgoa).

I note incidentally for occultists how *Nagualism* differs exactly from *Lycanthropy*. The *werewolf* is merely the objectification of the erratic astral body of a sorcerer in catalepsy; whereas the *Nagual* is a being perfectly distinct from the Mexican sorcerer, a being of inferior species, but to which he is bound by a chain of solidarity which have clear consequences and seems unquestionable.

NAHEMAH. – Queen of the Striges, in the Cacopneumatic of the Rabbis, and one of the four wives of *Sammael* (see this word).

NENUPHAR. – The anaphrodisiac properties of white nenuphar (*Nymphea alba*) are certainly magical; for they come precisely, like those of *Oak Mistletoe* (see this word), from the influences of stars in effective conjunction, at the hours when the plant is gathered and the philtre is prepared.

By itself, nenuphar is only endowed with banal emollient and sedative virtues, due to the mucilage it contains in abundance. But the charmers, experts in the works of ☽ and ♄ knew how to make ice-cold and frosty drinks, whose penetrating acuity numbs the most unbridled senses.

The Mystical Lotus of the Hindus, symbolising to a certain extent the blossoming of the Spiritual Essence in the silence of appeased passions, is a kind of nenuphar (Padma).

NUMBERS. – There is a science of numbers, whose mysteries are due to the most sublime arcane of transcendental magic. The language is lost for the modern man. But there are also many superstitions relating to numbers, and these are related to witchcraft (see any *Grimoire*).

O

OD: The odic force, or od force, is the name given to a hypothetical vital force or energy put forward by the German Karl von Reichenbach in the mid-19th century. The term is derived from the Norse mythological god Odin.

OAK MISTLETOE. – Mistletoe is a parasitic plant which attaches itself like a plant polyp to the branches of certain trees, especially oak, pumping out the superabundant vitality of the sap.

The Druids harvested it with a golden serpent at certain times and composed a prodigiously powerful elixir from its juice, rich in magnetic qualities. Mistletoe performed miracles in their hands, for they were magicians. – In the hands of sorcerers, who wanted to exploit it in their turn, this vampiric plant never gave anything but harmful or derisory results.

Fabre d'Olivet tells us that Ram, the theocrat of the migrating Hyperboreans, owed to a divine revelation the art of extracting a remedy from oak mistletoe, which cured Elephantiasis, that terrible evil, the exterminating scourge of the Celtic races, for a few days, and which was then considered incurable (see the *Hist. philos, du genre humain* (Philosophical history of mankind), volume I).

M. de Saint-Yves, who confirms this tradition, adds that the true Mistletoe, already very difficult to discern from similar parasites, only displayed its marvellous virtue when harvested under certain conditions, at a precise astronomical hour –see the *Mission des Juifs* (Mission of the Jews.

The progress of magnetism will one day lead to the discovery of the absorbent properties of Oak Mistletoe. The secret of these spongy growths, which attract the unnecessary luxury of plants and become overloaded with colour and flavour, will then be revealed; mushrooms, truffles, tree galls, the different species of mistletoe, will be used with discernment by a new medicine by dint of being old. Paracelsus will no longer be laughed at, as he used to collect the *usnea*[12] from the skulls of the hanged men… But one must not walk faster than science; it only moves backwards to better advance." –Eliphas Lévi, *Historie de la Magie* (History of Magic).

OBI (Mandigoës). – Formidable occult power, which is decimating the population of the West Indies.

P

PALINGENESIS: The process of bringing about the appearance of the form of a body after its destruction; i.e. a new or second birth or production; the state of being born again; regeneration.

PACT. – It is a contract, express or tacit, but freely consented to by both sides, between the Devil and the Sorcerer.

---

12 Usnea is a genus of mostly pale grayish-green fruticose lichens that grow like leafless mini-shrubs or tassels anchored on bark or twigs.

PEGS. – Sorcerers used wooden or metal pegs, which they stuck, with imprecations, into the wall nearest the victim chosen as target for their evil spell. The rather unexpected effect of this operation was, it is said, to provide urine retention. People sometimes died from this spell, according to Wuecker.

The Grimoires said that to obviate this spell, one only had to spit in one's right shoe before putting it on!

PERFUMES. – Perfumes, says Agrippa (*Philos, occulte*, book III, chap. LXIV) attract spirits "as a magnet attracts iron." They are used in cult ceremonies and in magical operations.

This is why the Sorcerer, always trying to imitate the priest and the magician, does not fail to use it for his evocations. Since sweet perfumes have an evocative virtue in the sphere of pure Spirits, it seems analogical to him to evoke impure Spirits by the effusion of the most unfortunate odours. He preferably uses the stinking fumigations of Saturn, which according to Eliphas Lévi (*Rituel...* (Transcendental Magic Its Doctrine and Ritual), chap. VII) are Dingridium, Scammonaeus, Alum, Sulphur and foul Asyssa. – See the word *Evocation*.

PHANTOM. – A generic name, designating any visible aggregate of molecules previously elusive to the eye, and suddenly compacted into the shape of a living being.

The classical Phantom is none other than the Ghost, that is to say the appearance of a deceased person, objectified from scratch: *Simulacrum vita carens*. Ghosts are, for the most part, nothing more than aromatic coagulations, dead or dying, – residues of astral shells in the process of disintegration in the fluidic ocean; perispirits[13] devoid of all consciousness, and which an external force has reacted to only for a fleeting existence.

When they manifest themselves, it is preferably around burials, slaughterhouses, amphitheatres, or even sewers and solfataras.

PHILTRES. – In Black Magic, philtres are drinks to disturb the psychic balance and to inspire delirious passions.

PHYLLOTAXIS. – Study of the arrangement and disposition of the leaves around the stem.

PHYLACTERIES. – See *Amulets* and *Talismans*.

PHYSIOGNOMY. – A particular aspect that, for each living being, results from all its parts, both internal and external. Character that distinguishes some

---

13 In Spiritism, perispirit is the subtle body that is used by the spirit to connect with the perceptions created by the brain.

things from all others. Aspect of a living being that makes it possible to evaluate it.

PINT. – Ancient measure for wine and other liquids. The pint of Paris was worth slightly less than a litre, i.e. 0.931 litres.

PLANETARY AND ZODIACAL SYMBOLS:

Sun	☉	Moon	☽ ☾ ⌒ ⌣	Mercury	☿	Venus	♀
Mars	♂	Jupiter	♃	Saturn	♄	Uranus	♅
Neptune	♆	Pluto	♇	Earth	⊕		
Aries	♈	Taurus	♉	Gemini	♊	Cancer	♋
Leo	♌	Virgo	♍	Libra	♎	Scorpio	♏
Sagittarius	♐	Capricorn	♑	Aquarius	♒	Pisces	♓

PSYCHURGY. – The action of man on the world of human souls. Psychurgy literally means: "action of the soul" (from the Greek *psuchê*, "soul", and *ergon*, "work").

PYTHONS. – Sacred serpents of Apollo, which coiled up on the arms of the Pythias, when they prophesied. Pythons were also called the Inspiring Spirits of the Sybil.

Q

QUEEN OF THE SABBATH. – She was usually the most beautiful. She had to be a virgin and sacrifice her modesty to the *Stinking Goat* (*sic*).

QUESTION. – Preliminary torture inflicted on defendants, to extract from them the confession of their crimes or the names of their accomplices.

R

RED DRAGON. – I have in front of me an obviously modern edition of this memorable grimoire. It is a clumsy reprint of the 1521 edition, and claims to pass for print the following year (1522).

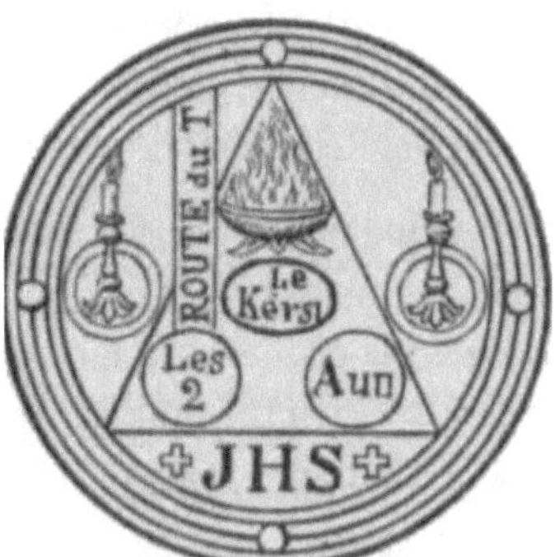

The Red Dragon
Magic Circle

The *Dragon rouge* (Red Dragon), or the art of commanding celestial, earthly, infernal spirits, etc. S. L., 1522, small in-12. (Decorated with a strangely naive frontispiece, printed in red, like the title).

The work will be judged by these lines, which open the first chapter. This great book is so rare, so much sought-after in our lands (sic) that, for its rarity, it can be called, according to the Rabbis, the true GREAT WORK; and it is they who have left us this precious original, which so many charlatans have wanted to forge needlessly by trying to imitate the real one, which they have never found,[14] so that you can catch money from the simple people who address the first person, without looking for the real source.

The Red Dragon
Frontispiece

---

14 This is what some people of bad company *call spitting in the air, so that the spit falls back on your nose…*

This one was copied from the true writings of the great King Solomon, which were found by pure chance, etc…

This is the first page of the Red Dragon. – *Ab una, disce omnes.*

RHOMBUS. – A sort of magic spinning top, with a monotonous humming, whose magnetic action is most powerful.

Hecate's Rhombus was one of the most famous among the witches of ancient Greece. It is mentioned in the oracular fragments attributed to Zoroaster: "Operare circa Hecaticum turbinem" (*De dæmonibus et sucrificiis*).

RINGS. – If it were a question of High Magic, I would speak of the *Ring of Solomon*, made of the seven mystical metals and provided with two kittens (one of moonstone with the star of the Macrocosm, the other of cornelian with that of the Microcosm), engraved with two hallmarks of gold and silver. For the details, I simply refer to the l'*Historie de la Magie* (History of the Magic) of Eliphas Lévi.

The *Ring of Gyges* or of invisibility, whose legend everyone knows, should not occupy us either.

A thousand extravagances are told about the wedding and engagement rings. Wizards advise husbands, when exchanging rings in front of the priest, to deliberately push the ring down to the root of their wives' fingers. For if the ring does not go lower than the second phalanx at that very minute, the wife takes ascendancy over her noble husband, whom she will turn into a fool and probably into a cuckold. Whereas, if the ring encircles the very root of the ring finger, the man will be the master of the house. Therefore, the Spell casters give young girls who feel a vocation to wear panties and relegate their master and lord to the third degree the perfidious advice to bend and stiffen their fingers during the ceremony.

It seems that superstitious, but far-sighted husbands could parry this manoeuvre by passing a ring of a monstrous diameter on the marital finger. – Unfortunately, the case is foreseen by the wily master of all prestige. The too wide ring is also symbolic of a disadvantage that husbands like to avoid. My modesty forbids me to say more. The rings are a kind of amulet or talisman, depending on the case.

S

SABBATH BOILER. – It is in an iron cauldron where the sorcerers and their companions reduce the broth of small children to a jelly-like consistency, with enchanted herbs and the venom of reptiles. – See Shakespeare (*Macbeth*, Act II).

SABBATH GOAT. – Favourite form borrowed by the prince of these congregations, whose name is Leonardo (see our chap. II).

It was reputed to be the fatal animal goat and sorcerer. Its blood was used in special compositions, in order to provide some terrifying visions.

This animal sometimes played the role of incubator. Thus we see in the Bible that some women of Israel abandoned themselves to the goats.

SABBATH. – Assembly of sorcerers and demons.

SACRAMENTS OF THE DEVIL. – Black Magic, this reverse religion, also has its sacraments, where one can distinguish, as in those administered by the Church, matter and form.

SACRIFICE. – Human sacrifices were universally accepted and passed into the mores of all the peoples of antiquity.

SALAMANDER. – A sort of lizard that lives in water, and was once considered to be endowed with the singular privilege of frolicking in the flame as in its element, and to stay there for a long time without the slightest discomfort. It is on the basis of this tradition, which was once universally widespread, that the neo-kabbalists named Salamanders the Elemental Spirits of Fire.

SAMMAEL. – This is, according to the Talmudists, the male incarnation of *Leviathan* (see this word); they also qualify it as the *sinuous Serpent*, see chap. I. The Zohar attributes the sin of Eve to the seductions of Sammael. From the latter, the demonologers have made one of the princes of Hell.

SATAN. – The fallen angel, the Devil.

SATYRES. – Country deities of the heathens.

The first Fathers of the Church speak of them as real beings, in flesh and blood. St. Anthony (St. Jerome tells us), met a Satyr in the desert who offered him dates and asked him for prayers.

There has been much dispute over the question of the Satyrs. The controversy was fierce at all times. Some want to see monkeys; others claim that the Satyrs were only men of the woods, savages. Read the very curious work by F. Hédelin, unfortunately quite rare:[15] *Des satyres brutes, monstres et démon* (About satyrs, monsters and demons), of their nature and worship, against the opinion of those who considered Satyrs to be a species of men distinct and separate from the Adamites. (Paris, Buon, 1627, in-8.).

Needless to add that the Satyrs (goat-feet) are part of the menagerie of the Sabbath.

---

15 Reprinted by Lisieux, but in very small numbers.

SECRETS. – Occult remedies, composed of words and gestures, to cure all kinds
of diseases.

Wonderfully stupid formulas. Often the stingy peasants pay dearly for
them. They are the verbal expression of an influence that is transmitted,
from father to son, in certain families. It should be noted that if the owner
of the secret gives or sells it, he loses it for himself.

When it comes to witchcraft, faith does everything… However, the peas-
ant, who has paid twenty coins for some foolish recipe, will never doubt the
efficiency of such an expensive treasure. If the secret has cost him nothing,
it is much less valuable to him, and therefore less likely to work a miracle
in his hands.

I have seen shepherds "heal from the secret", in five or ten minutes, a cow,
a pig, a horse, suffering from desperate illnesses, and which the vet considered lost. – Curiously enough! The "healer of the secret" never accepts a
coin for the price of the cure he performs. He works for glory.

The *Grimoire of Honorius* contains a number of recipes for "healing secrets".
As it is very rare, I think it would be curious to copy one of them:

"Against the flow of the belly. – I entered the Garden of Olives and
met St. Elizabeth; she spoke to me about the flow of her belly, I asked her for
mercy for mine, and she ordered me to say three *paternosters* in honour of
God and three *Hail Mary* in honour of St. John (*sic*)… Say three *paternos-
ter* and three *Hail Mary*, as it is said above, and you will be healed." (*Grim.
d'Honorius*, Rome, 1760, in-12, p. 62).

This is a secret for healing oneself; but all the formulas for healing other
men or animals are more or less of this kind.

See also the word: *Strings of the winds*.

SHIRT OF NECESSITY. – We must not forget here the shirt nicknamed "shirt
of necessity", which the Germans call *Nothembd*, so celebrated by our ancestors and which they used to wear during the war against the blows of
stings, balls and cannonballs… Fat women used the same shirt to give birth
more fast and more comfortably.

"It had to be made on one of the nights of the Christmas week; so much so
that the virgins spun the linen in the name of the Devil, they unwound it;
they wove and sewed the shirt. They tied two heads to the chest: the one on
the right side had a long beard and was like a morion with a head; the other
on the left side was terrible to see, and had a crown like that of King Beelzebub. On each side of these two heads there was a cross and the whole shirt
covered the man from the collar to half the body with the sleeves." (Jean
Wier, *Hist., disputes et disc. des illusions et impostures des Diables* (Histories,

disputes and discussions of the illusions and impostures of the Devils), etc., with two dialogues by Erastus, Geneva, 1579, in-8, book V, chap. XVIII.)

SIGNATURES. – A natural external marking or symbolic appearance or characteristic of a plant, mineral, or other object or substance that indicates its special medicinal quality or appropriate use.

SIGNS. – The sign is, in Magic, the point of support required by the will to project towards a prefixed goal. The adequate is the sign is to the inner verb, the more perfect and therefore effective it is. The countersign is a parry, by means of an occult shield, which sends back to the aggressor the shock in return for the blow he has dealt.

SNAKE EGGS. – The snake, primarily a magnetic animal, lays eggs very rich in a mysterious substance, which the alchemists of a certain school called mercurial cerebrin. This substance cannot be used in metal work, because the ☿ is specified for the Animal Kingdom; but its presence, explaining the occult properties of snake eggs, justifies the sagacity of the Druids, who collected them with care.
The adepts of Black Magic are not unaware of these exceptional properties; they take advantage of them for their evil spells.

SORTILEGES. – Operations of Black Magic.

SPAGYRIA, SPAGYRIC. – Spagyria is a name given to the production of medicines from plants using alchemical procedures. These procedures include fermentation, distillation and the extraction of mineral components from plant ashes. This word is attributed to Paracelsus: *spagyria*, from the Greek *spaô*, "to extract" and *ageirô* to gather. It was used as a synonym for chemistry.

SPIRITISM. – Sort of religion, founded around the middle of the century, by Allan Kardec (pen name). Spiritist practices consist mainly in the evocation of the beloved dead. The ceremonial used for this purpose has nothing of that indelible stamp of greatness that still saves, in the eyes of the artist, the most sacrilegious rites of priestly antiquity. If our modern necromancers make the oracle of the tomb speak, it is through the ministry of sibylline hats, talking occasional tables and *revolving tables* (see this last word).

SPIRITS. – This is the name given to the invisible agents that manifest themselves by knocks in seances.

STILETTO, MAGIC. – The *Clavicules de Salomon* (Clavicles of Solomon) (Manuscript of 1641, in-4, already quoted) want you to make it yourself. The handle must be, like the blade, made of fine steel, studded with magic characters. The consecration of the "Stiletto" is the same as that of the *sword* (see this word). The scabbard will be made of a brand new piece of red taffeta.

STRINGS OF THE WINDS. – "… The peoples of Fionia, before their conversion to Christianity, sold the winds to the sailors, giving them a cord with three knots, and warning them that by untying the first knot, they would have a gentle and favourable wind, at the second knot, a more vehement wind, and at the third knot, an impetuous and dangerous wind." (*Olaüs Magnus*, translated by Dom Calmet, *Traité sur les apparitions des Esprits et sur les Vampire* (Treatise on the Appearances of the Spirits and on Vampires), Volume I, p. 250).

SUCCUBUS. – Demon or female ghost, which provokes dreams of lust in young men. See the words *Incubus* and *Ephialtes*.

SWORD. – The Magic Sword, says the Manuscript (already quoted) of *Solomon's Clavicle*, must be brand new; having washed it well with wine, in which you will mix a little of the blood of a white dove which will have been killed one Monday, at six o'clock in the morning, and after having wiped it with clean cloths, you will wait until Tuesday, at six o'clock in the morning, to take it in your hand, and say these words with great attention: *Agla, On, Pentagrammaton, On Athanatos,* etc. (follows the conjuration).

Afterwards you shall engrave or make to be engraved on it, with the chisel of art, at the same hour of six o'clock in the morning, the following characters and words:[16]

araritha

"And when you have done so, you shall cast incense that has been blessed, and say the prayer *Agla, On, etc.* (shown above), and then you shall put it in its sheath, which must be new, and keep it for the time of need."(p. 13 of the *Clavicle*).

SYLPHS. – Elves, or Elemental Spirits of the Air (doctrine of the neo-kabbalists, followers of Paracelsus and modern rabbis).

T

TACITURNITY (charm of). – When a sorcerer or witch denied his crime, he was laid bare; then, shaving or depilating all his body, a meticulous investigation was carried on it.

---

16 We have a specimen of the strange characters which fill these kinds of works; but it seemed good to us to leave it there, for this kind of reproduction.

Why was this done? – First, to find the *stigma Diaboli*, the Devil's signature… In these places, the skin, completely insensitive, could be perforated without flinching. This was no small task (see *Marks*).

Above all, however, before inflicting the *Question* (see this word) on the defendants, they tried to find out if they did not hide the *Charm of Taciturnity* in some fold of the flesh or nail; it was a sort of diagram, which had the occult virtue of suppressing all pain, to the point that the exhausted torturers asked for mercy before the patient had flinched.

TALISMAN. – It is a sign, a character or an image, consecrated according to art, in order to bring good luck in a given circumstance.

There are talismans for the acquisition of wealth, marked with the sign of ☉; talismans for Love, composed under the auspices of ♀; talismans of ♃, to dominate men and constrain fortune; talismans for bravery and victory, studded with the sign of ♂, and so on.

Some talismans claim to be of the high Kabbalah; others, like the *Devil's scapulars*, are of the lowest Goetia.

TARANTULA. – This very poisonous spider is quite common in Southern Italy. It is said that those who are bitten by it, rush, it is said, in an interminable outburst of frenetic dance. The venom of the Tarantula was once part of some Neapolitan sorcerers' compositions.

TAROT (or BOOK OF THOTH). – Hieroglyphic instrument of the ancient Wise Men, later to become the instrument par excellence of *divination* (see this word); finally degenerated into a simple card game. Court de Gébelin, in his great work (*Le Monde Primitif* (The Primitive World), 1777, 9 vols. in-4), attributes the invention of the Tarot to the magicians of Egypt. Others trace it back to the primitive cycles of India, this ancient teacher of Mitzraim: a constant tradition among certain tribes of nomadic gypsies from the high Himalayan plateaus, who passed on –from time immemorial and from father to son– the divinatory art, inseparable from his prestigious instrument. The Tarot is essentially composed of twenty-two magic keys, figurative of the XXII Arcana of the Absolute Doctrine; and of for suits of fourteen cards, each one marked with a tetragrammatic sign: of the *Staff* (י, Yod ♃, Male Principle, Common *Clubs*); – of the *Cup* (ה, He ☿, Female Faculty, Common *Hearts*); – of the *Sword* (ו, Vav ♆, lingamic union of the two combined virtues, Common *Spades*); – finally of the *Sicle* or *Denarius* (ה, second He □, or ♁ fruit of this union, Common *Diamonds*).

Every suit of fourteen cards is made up of the *Pythagoras Denary* (Θ or θ, or 10, ספרוח *Sephiroth* of the Kabbalists), and a Quaternary[17] of emblematic figures, representing the application of the great Name or Scheme יהוה to each of the dynasties (the King is י ♉, the Queen ה ☿, the Knight ו ⚎ and the Valet ה Θ).

For further details, please consult Papus' very rich and complete work, the *Tarot des Bohémiens* (Tarot of the Bohemians).[18] Of all the occultists who have dealt with Thoth's book, Papus is the first to have the boldness and talent to scientifically deduce the law that governs the march of the Tarot. No one has gone further along this fruitful path.

Many editions of the Tarot are known; some of them are fundamentally altered in the figures, to the point of being unrecognisable. Examples: the German and Chinese Tarot cards, and the so-called Eteilla's corrected deck. Several others offer very notable variants. The most recommendable editions, with regard to the Magic Synthesis, are the so-called Besançon and Marseille editions, especially the last one. However, they cannot be said to be satisfactory…

It was expedient to rebuild at least the authentic edifice of the XXII Keys. Mr. Oswald Wirth bravely undertook this arduous task: by substituting correct drawings for the shapeless colourfulness of the old Tarots, this young initiate did a most meritorious job.[19] All lovers of Theosophy are now familiar with the Tarot de Paris, where the symbolism of the XXII Keys has been restored to its original purity by Mr. Wirth.

In the hands of the magician, the Tarot is a philosophical machine, revealing an absolute Synthesis. In the hands of the gypsies and the card-pullers, it is a mediator of divinatory lucidity; and since, through a dark alchemy, perverts know how to spoil the best things, *–optimi corruptio pessima–* the Tarot degenerates only too frequently, in the hands of modern sorcerers, into a very lucrative instrument of blackmail and even crime.

By inverting the four letters of the hierogrammatic word Taro, one obtains the sacred words: *Ator, Rota, Tora.*

TAUROBOLY. – Mysterious sacrifice of Mithraic origin; referred to the cult of Cybele by the Romans.

The priest immolated the sacred bull with a single blow of the priestly sword and, rushing under the warm fountain he had just opened, dipped

---

17 Tetractys of Pythagoras.

18 Paris, Carré, 1889, large in-8, fig. – See; on Papus and his works, our *Seuil du Mystère* (Mystery Threshold) (2nd edition).

19 See the *XXII Clefs du Tarot de Wirth* (XXII Keys of the Wirth Tarot) (Poirel, publisher, 1889).

his lip first of all in it, invoking the gods; then he stretched his shoulders to the mantle of living purple, which the sacramental sprinkling was going to cover it.

When the Emperor Julian wanted to make himself present and propitious to the gods of his old-fashioned Olympus, he consumed the sacrifice of the Tauroboly. Then, blinded by the blood that flooded him and suffocated by the fetidity of his steamy vapour, he saw the dethroned larvae of ancient Polytheism appear when he got up; pale and silly ghosts, fearful shadows that flee in light volutes at the sole sign of the cross, like those inconsistent morning mists, suddenly vanished at the first ray of sunlight.

TEETH. – The *Teeth* compete with hair and nail clippings for priority in the composition of spells.

TERAPHIM – This is how the hieroglyphic and priestly oracle of the ancient Hebrews was called. This oracle answered the questions of the high priest with *Urim* אורים and חוסים *Thummim*; toda we would say by tossing a coin. For the false *Teraphim*, see the words *Android* and *Mandrake*.

TEUTAD (or TEUTATES) and THOR. – Two fierce deities of the ancient Celtic. Human blood was annually shed as a sacrifice on their altars, lost in the sacred depths of the sounding forests –*luca sonantia late*.

TOAD. – One of the animals most often cited in the Grimoires.
It is certain that the mere sight of a toad produces a rather intense magnetic effect on impressionable people; it is believed in the countryside that it is enough to be fixed by this animal with a little persistence to fall into syncope.
Sorcerers seek for their charms the *Crapaudine*, a kind of stone which is said to be found in the heads of some toads.

TRANSPORT (FOR THE SORCERERS TO THE SABBATH). – This is what, in the East of France, is called *High-Hunt* (see this word).

TURNTABLES and **TALKING TABLES**. – This is modern witchcraft: I mean Spiritism and Spiritualism.
What, in reality, is *Spiritism* (see this word)? – It is the art of getting in touch with vampiric entities, elementals, larvae, etc…, which swarm in the intersidereal space and sometimes give a fleeting appearance of life to empty and dying astral shells, aerial corpses in the process of disintegration.
Does this mean that we deny any possibility of relations with higher Spirits, and even souls reintegrated by death into the kingdom of ethereal cosmogonic substance, of which our world is the material excrement? – Certainly not. Only it seems to us that, within the species, the Spiritists or Spiritual-

ists, with the best will in the world, evoke nine hundred and ninety-nine times out of a thousand ambiguous, evil, stupid and brutal beings.

TYING OF THE AGLET. – Means to cast a spell that was believed to have the power to prevent the consummation of marriage, making the man impotent (in French *Nouer l'aiguillette*).

U

UNDINES. – Elemental spirits of water, according to the eclectic doctrine of the neo-cabbalists. See what the Abbot of Villars says about it, in his *Comte de Gabalis* (Count of Gabalis).

UPAS. – From this tree (very common in the Maluku and Sunda archipelagos), the naturals know how to extract one of the most fearsome poisons known. Generally, the poisonous preparation itself is given the name *Upas*. There are two Upas, also toxic: *Upas antiar*, extracted by incision from an Urticea (*Antiaris toxicaria*), and *Upas tieuté* (*Tsettick* of the Javanese) which is prepared by reducing the bark of a liana (*Strychnos tieuté*) to the consistency of an extract. – Monographers have mistakenly confused these poisons with the famous Curare.

Muslim tradition says that the Upas trees miraculously came out of the soil of Java, under the curse of the prophet, and for the punishment of the infamous vice so common in Malaysia.

In the tormented centuries of the Middle Ages and the Renaissance, the adepts of poisonous magic, Genoese or Florentines, made these poisonous and subtle juices from tropical vegetation come back at a high price: they had the use of them.

URINE. – Sorcerers agree in proclaiming that the urine of a little boy or a young virgin is a marvellous specific for all kinds of illnesses, such as ringworm, mumps, rheumatism…

The marvellous virtue of urine, beaten according to the rite, to excite rain and storms.

USNEA. – Paracelsus, who has done wonders with the *Usnea*, defines it as a *kind of extremely spongy and tenuous tartar*, which is found on certain woods and on certain animal substances after decomposition. Legend has it that he would even collect it from the skulls of the hanged men; it was used to make up sympathetic remedies of incomparable virtue.

V

VAMPIRES. – Astral entities which, surviving the mortal remains of certain individuals, delay indefinitely their molecular disintegration. These pseudo-animal entities, united to the corpse by an invisible umbilical link, become erratic and attack the sleeping living. Vampirism is, so to speak –a posthumous, hereditary, often epidemic disease–.

VITZLIPUTZLI. – The God-snake of the Aztecs, whose idol is periodically sprinkled with bloody libations.

VOLT. – Wax figurine, modelled in the resemblance of the one you want to bewitch. By extension, any spell that is intended to bring death or illness, by virtue of magical execution.

VOODOO. – Wizards of the West Indies, fanatical sectarians of the snake-god, Voodoo.

VULNERARY. – Useful for healing wounds; adapted to the healing of external injuries: as, vulnerary plants or potions.

W

WAND. – It cannot be a question here about the *Wizard's Wand*, a magnetic steel rod, imprisoned in an almond tree branch, which carries a small crystal lance at one end and a small resin lance at the other. In addition, Eliphas Lévi treats them knowledgeably in the *Rituel de la Haute Magie* (Transcendental Magic Its Doctrine and Ritual).
Sorcerers also have their Wand, with which they draw the *magic circle* (see this word) and claim, in their overconfidence, to dominate the elements. "This wand must be of hazel –says Collin de Plancy–, and of the shoot of the year. It must be cut on the first Wednesday of the Moon, between eleven o'clock and midnight, while pronouncing certain words. The knife must be new and kept above, when cutting. Then the wand is blessed; the word AGLA + (אגאלא) is written on the large end, in the middle ON + (און) and TÉTRAGRAMMATON + (יהוה) on the small end; and it is said: *Conjuro te cito mihi obedire... etc.....*"(*Dictionnaire Infernal* (Infernal Dictionary).
Other wizards, more astute, rim the branch at both ends, with the steel of the blade used to cut the branch; then they magnetised these two ironed ends. Finally, they rub the small end with blood, and soak the big end in urine where they have extinguished a firebrand. – These various rites, observed by the witch rabbis of Alsace, are extremely remarkable from an analogical point of view; they bear witness to a real science, deviated to the left.

WATER. – Witches have been accustomed to beating the water with rods; summoning demons. This small operation is intended to excite storms and hail, or to make heavy rain fall.

Water was once used for trials. People suspected of witchcraft were thrown into the river. If they drowned, they were considered innocent; if, on the other hand, they were found floating, it was an infallible indication of their guilt. In this case, they were burned. An attractive alternative!

Boiling water was also used for trials. The accused had to plunge his hand into a boiler placed on an inferno, and bring back a blessed ring, suspended by a wire between two waters.

WEREWOLVES. – "In Sorcery, men and women who have been metamorphosed or who metamorphose and transmute themselves into wolves, are called Werewolves" –Collin de Plancy, *Dictionnaire infernal* (Infernal Dictionary)–.

WHITE MICE. – Some sorcerers, and notably a miserable renegade priest who has passed away, with weapons and baggage, in the service of Satan, still consummate spells, by slitting the throats of white mice, which they feed with consecrated hosts.

This mode of *bewitchment* (see this word) is traditional among a corrupted fraction of the Roman clergy.

Scientific Name Plant Index

U

V